THE
WEIMARANER
TODAY

Vicky Bambridge

Ringpress

Published by INTERPET PUBLISHING
Vincent Lane, Dorking, Surrey, RH4 3YX
United Kingdom

First Published 1991
Reprinted 1996, 2002
Third edition published 1999
© 1999 RINGPRESS BOOKS
& Vicky Bambridge

ISBN 1 86054 101 1

Printed and bound in Singapore
by Kyodo Printing Co

10 9 8 7 6 5 4 3 2 1

This book is dedicated to Mr Harvey

Contents

Sh. Ch. Hansom Portman of Gunalt: Winner of 22 CCs and the only Weimaraner to go Best in Show at an All Breeds Championship Show.
Owned by Mr and Mrs S. A. Hollings. Bred by Mr R. M. W. Finch.

INTRODUCTION

The Weimaraner, or Grey Ghost, comes from Weimar, a republic of Germany. It was originally bred to hunt deer and wild boar, and to protect its owner in times of danger. The breed's hunting instinct has remained of prime importance, and in Germany dogs are still used to track game that has been injured in road accidents, and they are also used to compete in Schweiss Trials – a tracking test using a blood scent. The breed was exported, and the first Weimaraners arrived in Britain in 1952. The attractive and unusual appearance of these dogs, coupled with their intelligence and versatility, soon made them a much sought-after breed, and dogs were imported from America, and from other European countries. Today, most Weimaraners in Britain are home-bred, although selected imports have been introduced from abroad to revitalise bloodlines.

The Weimaraner is a most versatile breed, and it is used for hunting, pointing and retrieving, agility competitions and obedience work. In the last few years Weimaraners have gained ground competing in Field Trials, and some are now being used on shoots for their ability in finding and retrieving game. They have been particularly successful in Working Trials, and Weimaraners have competed successfully against other breeds for the top honours in this sport. In the show ring, the Weimaraner is becoming increasingly popular and has become one of the leading Gundog breeds; entries at shows are getting bigger, and registrations with the Kennel Club are growing. In 1989 the breed reached a milestone in Britain when a

Weimaraner went Best In Show at an All Breeds Championship Show, and in 1991 a Weimaraner was the Reserve Group winner at Crufts Centenary Show.

The growth of popularity within a breed must always be regarded as a mixed blessing, for it is important that the dog remains true to its original type, both in appearance and temperament. The Weimaraner is no exception, and the breed's intelligence and learning ability can lead to problems if it is handled incorrectly. This applies to the males in particular, as they can become a dominant member of the family if they are given an opportunity, rather than being content with a subservient role. However, when a Weimaraner is well trained and obedient, it is a tremendously rewarding dog. If this is the breed for you, I hope this book will help you to care for your dog, to train it in whichever field you wish to specialise, and perhaps most important of all, to enjoy your Weimaraner as a loving and loyal companion.

Chapter One

BUYING A PUPPY

When you have decided that a Weimaraner is the breed for you, the next step is to find out where to obtain a dog. You have several choices: you can write or telephone the national Kennel Club and request a list of breeders and the addresses of breed clubs; you can contact a dog agency – addresses can usually be found in veterinary surgeries or in Yellow Pages; or you can reply to advertisements in your local newspapers. However, it is worth doing a little research on the breed before you contact a breeder. A breed club will supply you with a copy of the Breed Standard, and this will give you an idea of what a good specimen should look like, and what faults to look out for. Go to some shows that have Weimaraner classes scheduled, and then you will have the opportunity to see the different types within the breed, and you can find out who breeds them.

It is wise to contact several breeders, including those that are not in your area, in order to obtain an average price. This will also help you to gain more experience of the breed, and you will find out what interest the breeder has in their stock once it has been sold. When you think you have found the right person, make an appointment to visit the kennels. It is essential to inform the breeder what you want your puppy for – whether it is for show or work, or perhaps as a future brood bitch. The breeder will then be able to advise you which puppy is suitable. If you require a puppy for show it must have a good mouth with a perfect scissor bite. The teeth may appear very small on some puppies, or even half-hidden by the gums, but the bite will never change. When the milk teeth fall out they will be replaced by adult teeth, and if the teeth are crooked and the mouth is undershot or overshot, it will never improve. The front of the puppy should be straight. If you hold up a puppy of six to eight weeks its feet will fall slightly away from each other. However, if you place the puppy on a table so that it is standing square, it will give you a good indication if the front is good. Most puppies will stand nice and square at an early age, and so it is well worth trying this little test – the puppy will not mind at all! The same applies to the rear, which should be square to the front. I remember someone once saying a Weimaraner should be like a table – it should have a leg at each corner and this is quite a good analogy. The dog should be balanced at a very young age. Watch the puppy as it runs freely up and down. It should not throw its feet out, and its elbows should be well tucked in. The breeder will be able to pick out a puppy with show potential, but there can be no guarantee that it will become a top winner. A lot depends on the way you feed, exercise and train your dog.

If you require a dog for work, either as a rough shooting dog, or for working tests, field, or obedience trials, soundness is of paramount importance. There is no point in training a dog for two years if it is unsound. It is therefore best to buy from stock which is both hip-scored and eye-tested. Again, there is no guarantee that your dog will not suffer from these problems, but it certainly reduces the risk. Some kennels have several generations tested, and these are obviously to be recommended. Eye problems are prevalent in the breed, and so it always wise to purchase from stock that has been tested. If your Weimaraner is going to work it should be outgoing in personality and unafraid of loud noises. Never buy a shy or retiring puppy for work – go for the one that is extrovert and inquisitive. If you are looking for a future brood bitch, the puppy you purchase must be the soundest you can find. Ideally, she should be line bred (this is explained more fully in the Chapter on Breeding), so you can predict the type of Weimaraner she will produce. Every kennel has its type – different heads, colour and body height – all within the Breed Standard. The bitch is certain to have some faults, so try to assess these, as they will certainly appear in her offspring. That is why soundness is so important. The purchase of a brood bitch is a big step for anyone, so take time to study the breed before you commit yourself. Unfortunately, some people are reluctant to tell you whether they plan to show or work their puppy, as some breeders charge more for certain puppies. However, if the puppies are well bred and conform to the Breed Standard, they should fit any

Weimaraner puppies sired by Ch. Varstock Voyager of Roxberg – typical specimens of the breed.

purpose. If the litter has serious faults either in bone structure, temperament, colour or hereditary disorders, then do not buy. There is no shortage of litters on the market, so take the time to find the right puppy.

When you first visit a breeder, it is best to go when there are no puppies available. This may sound silly, especially if you have to travel a long distance, but it is very easy to fall in love with a beautiful silver puppy with the sad blue eyes, and you will not make a balanced assessment of the stock. The more time you spend in finding the right animal, the more beneficial it will prove to be later on. The average life span for a Weimaraner is ten years, so you are going to have your dog a long time. Be punctual in keeping your appointment – breeders have to abide by strict feeding times with young stock; and remember that you are going to visit dogs – not going to a disco, so wear something sensible. I remember one lady who turned up wearing a crisp white jumper and matching jeans. She left with lovely designer paw marks evenly distributed on her lovely outfit, though she did praise the friendliness of our dogs! If you are purchasing a puppy as a family pet, it is important that you take the children along to visit the breeder. This will enable you to judge the temperament of the dogs and the children's reactions to the dogs. Some children are frightened of large dogs, and several visits to the breeder can build up their confidence. The dogs should be outgoing and friendly; they should not show any aggression and they

A Weimaraner puppy ready to leave its mother and littermates.

should welcome visitors quite happily. If the breeder has puppies, the bitch should still receive visitors happily with her offspring. A bitch will only protect her litter if she feels threatened. She should never need to be shut away in order for you to see her puppies. If you have any doubts, do not buy.

The puppies' mother should look in good coat, and she should be well-covered, with no tendency towards appearing thin or drained. She will, of course, have large milk teats which will make her look like a nanny goat, but more importantly she should appear happy and well. Look out for runny eyes, colds, or skin complaints in the puppies and the adults; make sure there is no evidence of underweight dogs with ribs showing through, and take note of the general hygiene in the kennels. But remember that kennels do not have to be the latest models in order to be clean and tidy.

Hopefully, you will be able to see several generations of dogs, and then you can judge temperament, colour and type at all stages. This is particularly important if you are planning to show your puppy. Never buy a puppy because you feel sorry for it. If the bitch is in poor condition and the puppies are anxious and poor-looking, go elsewhere! You will not be helping the situation. In fact, you are far more likely to improve matters if you refuse to buy, and the breeder has difficulty selling his puppies: he may not be so anxious to breed a litter next time. Puppies which are not

An eight-week-old puppy settles happily into its new home.

looked after properly from birth can develop serious problems later in life. They should be bright-eyed and have plenty of bounce. They should not be nervous and try to shy away from you. Their skin should be elastic and fall well into place around the body. It should feel soft, sleek and silky. Nails should be short and ears should be clean. Take your time and inspect the puppies thoroughly. Check for any hernia cuts, bruises, skin disorders, or sores, and make sure the eyes are both the same colour. A Weimaraner's eyes are blue at birth and they change as the puppy matures. An infection at an early stage could upset the colour balance, thus producing eyes of a different colour. This is obviously no use if you require a show dog. The eyes should fit the sockets well, the rims should not be baggy or droopy, and they should be the same colour as the coat – not bright pink. Weimaraners are prone to an eye condition called entropion, and stock with this disorder should never be bred from, and should not be shown.

A puppy should look happy and healthy, and it should run freely with its littermates. Check to make sure the puppies have been wormed. By the time the pups are eight weeks old they should have been wormed at least once. I worm my puppies twice: once at three weeks and again at six weeks, which ensures that the host has been removed. Find out how many times the puppy will require feeding, so you can arrange your timetable before the puppy arrives home. You should receive a diet sheet with your puppy, and it is best to keep to this, at least for the first few days. Breeders can spend years perfecting diets to suit their stock, and a change in diet, water and environment can upset a youngster. The puppies should be fully weaned (not requiring their mother's milk) at seven weeks of age. They will usually be receiving four meals a day. It is important that your puppy is fed at the same times every day. It is like a baby and requires a strict feeding routine.

Before you bring your puppy home, you must work out how you are going to cope with the newcomer. Is it going to be allowed to lie on the sofa, and sleep on the bed? If you do not want this type of behaviour you must establish what it is allowed to do right from the start. The puppy must have its own bed, and this should be in a quiet place where it can retreat for periods of rest without being disturbed. To start with, a cardboard box with a woolly jumper inside is perfectly sufficient. Expensive beds can be ruined by a chewing puppy, and as your dog will grow so fast it is easy to purchase the wrong size. You will also need to buy two feeding bowls. We have found the stainless steel type are the best. They last a lifetime and they are easy to clean.

House training is also an important consideration. Puppies cannot go for long periods without relieving themselves, and so if the dog is to be left on its own for any length of time, leave it somewhere where it can do the minimum amount of damage. A small puddle on the kitchen floor is not too bad, but if a puppy has the scope to explore, a small pile of faeces can become a horrendous series of paw prints. You would not leave a toddler alone for too long, and the same applies to your puppy. Decide who is going to train the puppy: it is less confusing for the puppy if you stick to one person.

All puppies need toys to play with, but you must decide which are their toys, and everything else is out of bounds. This is very important if there are young children in the family, as there is nothing worse than a favourite toy disappearing down the garden on a muddy day. If you are away from home for long periods of time you will need a kennel. This will enable you to enjoy your dog when you have time, and the dog will not become bored, as it would if it was left alone in the house. All dogs love to watch what is going on, and it will be far more content if it is left in a kennel and run. Weimaraners like their own bit of space and they adapt to living in a kennel very well. You can always have the dog in the house when you are around to supervise it. Finally, you will need to find a good vet in your area, so you can take your new puppy to be checked over and to be advised about inoculations. The puppy will be open to all infections until it has received its inoculations, and it must therefore be kept away from other dogs and places such as parks, which are used by other dogs. Most vets will vaccinate at ten to twelve weeks, though in heavily populated areas some will prefer to do it at eight weeks. The inoculations will protect the puppy against distemper, hepatitis, leptospirosis and parvovirus. The vet gives initial injections, and the course is completed two weeks later. It may be advisable to ask your vet about a cough vaccination, as this infection can spread quickly and could put your dog out of the show ring or working field for anything up to four weeks, in severe cases. Prevention is better than cure. The cost of vaccinations varies from area to area, and so do vet's charges, so it is worth making enquiries. However, the most important thing is to find a vet that specialises in small animals, and one that you are happy with. When you have found a vet, it is worth staying with the practice as they will keep a full record of your dog's health, which is beneficial to all parties. Weimaraners are usually very good and calm when visiting the vet – they seem to enjoy all the extra attention!

Now the big day has arrived and you are ready to collect your puppy. You should also receive a pedigree signed by the breeder. Without the pedigree your puppy is a mongrel. The puppy should be registered by the Kennel Club, and you may receive this certificate on the day of collection, or it may be posted on later. Some breeders also insure their puppies, and they will issue a cover note for this. I always do this, as puppies can be very accident-prone in their first few weeks in a new home. It is worth preparing a check-list before you go to collect your puppy, as it can save any misunderstandings at a later stage. Make sure you are completely happy with your puppy, and if you have any queries do not be frightened to ask. Equally, never be afraid to change your mind – this is is your decision and you must live with the consequences. However, most breeders are only too happy to try and correct any problems that may arise with training or settling in, long after the puppy is sold. Make sure you have a receipt, and the breeder's address and telephone number. The breeder can teach you a lot about the breed: they can advise about health matters and training, and they can help you if you want to enter the world of competition with your dog.

Early days: A lot of patience is needed when you start training a puppy.

Chapter Two

BASIC TRAINING

All dog owners and breeders have their own ideas about training puppies and adult dogs. This chapter is intended as a guideline, based on our training methods which have been tried and tested over many years.

Training starts the day you collect your puppy. If it is a puppy of your own breeding, the first lessons should start at approximately eight weeks of age. If you have bred the puppy you have one advantage as it will already know your voice. Voice is the most important element in training and the differing pitches of voice should provoke different reactions in your youngsters. You must therefore adopt different voices for commands. If you are praising your pup, the voice should be lighter, jolly and excitable. If you are giving a command such as 'sit', 'stay' or 'down', the voice should be firm and forceful, but you do not have to shout. The dog will respond to a stern, deep voice when it has been trained. As a bundle of eight weeks your puppy will be a lovable comedian, but habits that are amusing in a puppy can be intolerable in an adult. All puppies love to chew, and they will not discriminate over their choice of object. If you do not intervene at an early stage it could result in the best sofa being chewed when the pup gets older. So let your puppy have a toy to amuse itself with, and then remove it when the game is over, putting it away somewhere high up. If the puppy touches anything else, a sharp 'no!' and 'leave!', at the same time pulling your puppy away, should soon break the habit. You must be persistent, as the puppy will certainly be; but it is amazing how quickly it will learn to react to the voice used sternly.

If you watch your puppy moving around the room, you can learn a great deal. If it needs to pass water or open its bowels it will probably walk around more quickly, as if looking for something. In this instance, I pick the puppy up and quickly put him outside, via the front door. Always use the same door, and remember, to begin with, puppies do not know the layout of your house so they do not know where the front door is. If you keep an eye on your puppy and it is put out at the right time on several occasions, it will soon get the message. When the puppy is outside, let it wander around for a little while until you are quite sure it has finished its business.

Some household articles can be dangerous to a puppy intent on investigating everything it comes across. I had a dog who loved underwear, and any items left on radiators would disappear. This was alright until he got hold of a pair of tights which got stuck in his throat. I remember pulling them out, which was a most unpleasant job, but it could easily have been much worse. Do not let your puppy play with the children's toys – it could have worms – and do not let it lick the baby. Puppies love babies: they are often sticky and smell of food, and toddlers are often carrying biscuits and other treats around at nose-level – to your puppy these are a wonderful temptation. However, children and Weimaraners usually mix well and I have never heard of any dog of this breed that disliked children. In order to build up a good relationship children must be taught to respect the dog and not to be cruel. If the puppy is sleeping, it must be allowed to sleep in peace. The puppy must also learn respect: nipping must be stopped at an early age. This can be done either by tapping sharply on the nose with a rolled-up newspaper, or by using your hand. This may sound harsh, but this habit has to be stopped as soon as it starts.

When your puppy has settled in, and is becoming cleaner in the house and is more responsive, you can start lead-training. I usually embark on this at approximately nine weeks of age, and I use a webbing lead, which is soft and has a ring at one end (a slip lead). The first step is to take the puppy somewhere safe like the garden, where the grass is soft and non-slippery, and slip the lead over itshead. Hold the lead firmly, but not tightly, and walk off calling the puppy's name, putting gentle pressure on the lead. You will probably find to begin with that the puppy will resist, doing somersaults and cartwheels, and pulling in the opposite direction. Ignore all this, and call the puppy, talking to it and encouraging it as you gently pull the lead. As you walk on, it will soon get the message. If you have another dog the puppy will probably follow it quite happily; some will also follow a child. Once the puppy has decided it has no other choice than to go with you, it will settle and return to its normal self. It has to accept that you are in charge and it has to behave. This time spent with your puppy working on its basic training is the most important time of its entire education. Do not be tempted to rush through each stage of training, as your puppy can only accept so much at any one time. If you do force the pace, you will find that you will only have to return to the basics. When the puppy has got used to having a lead on, it will probably start to pull, but a gentle pull back at intervals will soon correct this tendency. Never allow your puppy to drag you along; if it is corrected when it is still young and small, it will not develop into a big problem.

By the time your puppy is twelve weeks of age and has completed its vaccinations, you will be itching to show your youngster to the world, although you will probably have had a flood of visitors to meet the newcomer in your home. A new puppy is like a magnet to dog lovers! If you have been doing basic training around the garden, then the puppy will be ready to go out. Never take a young puppy out near the road if it is not under proper control. It has almost certainly never seen a lorry before, never mind a tractor, and other agricultural machinery, which can appear forbidding to a youngster. Try not to expect too much from your puppy too soon. In time, walks will be enjoyable and your dog will be stimulated by all the new experiences. One of my youngsters found his walks very exciting and took in all his new surroundings with great interest. One day, as I was walking up our drive I saw a sheep, which had escaped from a nearby field. The dog was so excited at the prospect of a new playmate he could hardly contain himself – I am sure he thought it was a Standard Poodle! However, the sheep didn't look too amused, and it was a useful lesson in teaching the puppy that I was in charge, and he couldn't always please himself. When you meet other dogs it is wise to ask the owner if the dog is friendly. Puppies are very nosey and if your dog gets bitten it may become reluctant to mix with other dogs. This could make life very awkward if you intend showing or working your dog. It must socialise well; if it doesn't, it is better left at home.

When you are out walking with your dog, in the town or in the country, you must always be aware of it – watching out for its reactions and talking to it to keep its attention, and to reassure it. Simple things like a pheasant flying up out of a hedge can startle it. On no account should a youngster be allowed to chase game or other animals; this can be very dangerous, especially if it is near a road. If you see game or any other livestock, let the puppy look at it, and say 'leave' in a firm, forbidding voice. Stand there for a few minutes so the puppy can watch what it going on, and then you can praise it and continue your walk. In this way the dog will get used to seeing livestock without chasing it. If the puppy gets excited and starts barking, correct it with a jerk on the choke chain and say 'no' in a stern voice. You must be firm but kind with your Weimaraner to get the best out of it, and you must treat it with respect. You should think of it in the same way as a child: it can only absorb things for short periods, and it can forget what it has been taught quite easily – so be patient. The Weimaraner is a quick learner, and it can learn bad habits just as quickly as good ones, so be on your guard. How does it know if it is doing something wrong, unless it is corrected?

When you arrive at street corners and junctions, teach your puppy to sit, pulling gently on its lead and pushing down on its hindquarters. Wait a few seconds before moving off, and then give lots of praise. Weimaraners always attract attention, and so, if you meet other people in the street and stop to chat, make your dog sit and wait until it is time to move off. At home you can go further in your puppy's training with the 'sit and stay'. The puppy should be on a long lead – you can extend the ordinary lead with a piece of string – and you should start by commanding your puppy to sit. Then tell it to stay, and back away gradually, repeating the command 'stay' all the time. If the puppy tries to get up, put it back in position, and firmly tell it to 'stay'. When the puppy is staying in position, you can progress to the end of the lead. If it moves, do not get angry, just put the puppy back in position and start again. Do not over-do it – a ten minute training session is sufficient to begin with. The next step is to repeat the exercise with the puppy off the lead. Position the puppy on a marked spot, such as a chalked cross or circle. This may sound silly, but it is important to know that your dog has remained exactly in position, and not moved off its mark. Then turn your back on the puppy and walk forward a few strides. If the puppy has moved, go back and repeat the exercise, repeating the command 'stay' at frequent intervals. If – by a miracle – the puppy has remained in place, call it to you and give it lots of praise. This exercise should be repeated at every training session, gradually increasing the time and distance that you can leave your dog.

When you are out, your dog must be under control at all times. If you do not feel confident, do some more work at home, or join an obedience training class. When you are confident that your dog is responding to commands, you can let it off the lead. It is a good idea to start this at home in the garden with your dog walking to heel. Your dog should be used to walking to heel on the lead, and as most Weimaraners love to follow their owners, it should be relatively easy to encourage your dog to stay with you off the lead. Walk at a brisk pace, and command your dog by saying 'heel' or 'close', and slapping your thigh to keep the dog's attention. If the dog is not responding, put it back on the lead and do some heel work with it. The Weimaraner is very intelligent, and it should soon learn what is required. However, do not get too confident; your dog should be kept on a lead in all public places and whenever it is near a road. This is for its own safety. When your dog has mastered all the basic commands, you will have a well-behaved dog that you can take anywhere. You are now ready to progress to more specialised training, and if you have got the basic training right, your dog's further education should progress with little problem. If you do encounter any difficulties, return to the basics, and after a refresher course, your dog should be ready to proceed again.

All puppies should get used to travelling in cars, and again, this is important if you plan to show or work with your dog, as both pastimes usually mean a lot of lengthy car journeys. Before you set off on your first trip with your puppy, you must decide whereabouts it is going to travel in the car. You may have an estate car with a properly designed dog cage, but these are expensive for the pet owner. If your dog is well trained it will sit in any car without being caged, but it must be secure, and it must not be able to interfere with the driver. If the only place for the dog is on the back seat, then it must be tied up. A fully grown Weimaraner is a substantial weight, and if you had to brake sharply, the dog would be propelled into the front of the car. Before setting off on a journey, check to see if there are any wires hanging down; rear-heated window plugs make lovely chews. It is best to remove all temptation from a puppy by taping up any parts that could be chewed. The first time you take your puppy out, make sure you have plenty of newspaper; it may be sick or it may relieve itself, so cover the floor with papers, just in case. Whenever you go for a drive with your dog, take a bowl and a small bottle of water. In the summer it can be very hot travelling in the back of a car, and it is important to keep the dog's fluid levels up. If you are travelling a lot in summer, try to make your journeys at the cooler times of the day. If you decide to show your dog, you will be travelling early in the morning, depending where the show is. After the show, it is better to delay your departure until early evening, rather than have a frantic dog panting away in the back of the car. You will, of course, arrive home later, but after all, your dog has worked hard for you during the day.

The first time your puppy is in the car it will probably make a lot of noise; you must ignore this and it will soon stop. I usually turn up the radio, and this nearly always works. When you arrive at your destination, if it is not too hot, you should leave your dog in the car for about ten minutes until you have sorted yourself out. If the dog expects to be let out every time the car stops, it may bark and become a nuisance. It is far better that it is used to waiting its turn. All too often at shows I have seen dogs going mad in cars, not giving their owners time to organise themselves. But early training can prevent this problem from arising.

Your dog must learn good manners and respect, and it is up to you to teach it how to behave. There are no short-cuts; firmness, kindness and patience are the only methods that will work. A well-trained dog is a pleasure to own and hopefully, it is never a nuisance to anyone; as a result it will enjoy its life to the full. If you want more help in training your Weimaraner, contact a local training club. The Kennel Club or breed club can give you the necessary information – but don't leave it too late. Start training early and then your dog will never get into bad habits.

Chapter Three

CARING FOR YOUR WEIMARANER

FEEDING

Everyone has different ideas on feeding and rearing, and from youngster to veteran all dogs are individuals and require varying amounts of food and protein levels. With the enormous variety of complete foods and mixes available on the market it is very easy to be tempted to change from one diet to another. However, all changes in diet should be introduced gradually, perhaps over a period of seven days or more. Sudden changes can result in diarrhoea and loss of appetite. If this happens with a puppy it can put the growth pattern back, in severe cases for up to a month. For if a puppy loses condition it can take a long time to recover. Take time to analyse the feed you have decided to use, looking at the protein levels and comparing it with the amount of work your dog is doing. It is no use feeding a supercharged high-protein diet if your dog only gets a walk to the nearest shop and back. For the average dog at home with a daily walk you will probably find that 18 per cent to 24 per cent protein will be high enough. If your Weimaraner is highly strung and over-active then cut down its protein and increase its bulk, i.e. biscuits. If your dog is lethargic then do the opposite – put up its protein. Again any increase has to be assessed over a period of a week or more. Nowadays there are diets already manufactured for pet dogs and working dogs, which makes feeding easier. However, it may still take you time to find one that really suits your dog.

If you decide to feed a complete food, it means just that – you must not add meat, or anything else to it. A complete diet has been specially designed as such, and if you add to it, the balance will be upset. If you have any queries with any specific food, the feed company concerned will be only too happy to answer them. Dogs are not like humans – they do not require a wide variety of food at each sitting; they are quite happy on one balanced diet, even though it may be the same every day. You must feed at approximately the same time every day; this is important when keeping animals in peak condition. Get into a routine with your feeding, and stick to it. If you are away all day or you are away showing other dogs, then ask a friend to come in and feed at the appointed times.

If you have just purchased a puppy you should have received a diet sheet which you should follow, at least until the youngster has settled. Any changes should be discussed with the breeder. Remember, the puppy has had a change in environment and a change of water, so a sudden change in diet would be an added anxiety for your youngster. When your puppy is three to four months of age it will require worming again. Its food intake should gradually increase, and it should receive two meals a day. A calcium tablet should be added to its feed two to three times a week, depending on the amount of milk your puppy is receiving. This will help bone growth. However, too much calcium can be harmful, and so care must be taken when feeding vitamins and additives. As your puppy becomes older its eating habits will settle down and you will know by the amount left in the bowl whether you are feeding the right amount. If your dog is becoming too fat, you will need to cut down on its food.

It is not wise to give a puppy too much exercise. Some dogs are more active and lose weight quickly. If your puppy fluctuates in weight, and yet still seems to be eating well, then it may require worming. If you have wormed the puppy and you are still having problems, it may be worth having a word with your vet. Weimaraners can suffer from a pancreatic disorder, and changes in weight may be symptomatic of this condition. If your dog has had a hard season working, it may have lost a lot of weight, but it should return to normal when the season finishes. A stud dog will require extra protein if he is used a lot, in order to keep him in good condition – no one will want to use a skinny dog. A brood bitch will also require a special diet when she is in whelp and feeding her youngsters; again, specially designed complete diets are available from pet shops. Ask the breeder of your dog for advice, or anyone else that is experienced in the breed.

In the first six months of a puppy's life a balanced diet should be maintained, without introducing sudden changes, and the following rules should be adhered to:

Feed at approximately the same times every day.
Make sure water is available at all times.
Follow the manufacturer's instructions for serving, especially their guide
to quantities.
Worm your dog regularly; if in doubt, consult your vet.
Watch out for any changes in temperament – it may be due to diet.
Supplement vitamins and minerals only if they are not included in the food.

VETERANS: Dogs over seven years of age need as much care and attention as youngsters. As the dog ages it may have a tendency to lose weight, and so the diet should be higher in protein, with a little extra bulk, such as biscuits. Vitamin and mineral additives are essential in maintaining condition in a veteran. I use cod-liver oil, as I think this helps to keep the coat in good condition, and it can also help to ease stiffness in the joints, especially when the dog is over ten years of age. Of course, all veterans vary in how active they stay, and some will take on a new lease of life when a youngster is introduced to the home environment. The elderly dog still needs exercise, and while some may be happy to run around at home, it is better for those dogs that have been used to a hard working life to be kept to a normal exercise routine. Weimaraners can become very upset if they are suddenly left out of the limelight; they will sulk if they are not fussed over, so try to be tactful if you have other younger dogs that are vying for your attention. By the time your Weimaraner becomes a veteran you should know its likes and dislikes, and so there is no need to introduce any major changes in routine, unless the dog appears bored or is showing signs of fatigue. The main thing is to give lots of love and attention, in return for all the devotion your dog has given you.

GENERAL CARE

When you have decided where you are going to keep your dog, you must then ensure that it is safe and contented in its environment. If the dog is kennelled, it must be kept clean and you should adopt a routine with its kennelling. The kennel must be draught-proof and some bedding must be used. I use straw in winter; wheat straw is

The vet will give your dog a check-up when it has its annual booster inoculations.

the best, and it can be obtained from a farmer at a modest price. It should be shaken up when the dog is absent, and the dust should be allowed to settle before your dog returns. Wood shavings can be used in summer; they are little bit more expensive than straw, but they are ideal in hot weather. If your dog has eye problems it is best not to use straw or shavings as the dust can cause irritation. There are several varieties of shredded bedding on the market that may be more suitable.

A clean bucket containing fresh water should be placed in a corner of the run, out of the sunshine. If you have a dog who continuously tips over water buckets and bowls, then it is advisable to fix a bracket to the run or kennel in which a bucket can be placed. The water bucket has to be changed every day. I find it easier when cleaning out the kennels to swill out the run with the old drinking water, and refill with fresh water, which saves on the amount of water that is used. All feeding bowls must be collected after feeding, and a separate sponge or cloth should be used for cleaning the bowls. If feeding bowls are left with the dog, they can easily be damaged.

If your Weimaraner is kennelled, it must be let out for a run every day, otherwise it will become bored and this leads to destructive behaviour such as chewing up its kennel. Your dog should be allowed to have a good run to let off steam. If your dog is free-running off the leash, you must make sure it does not roam too far and cause

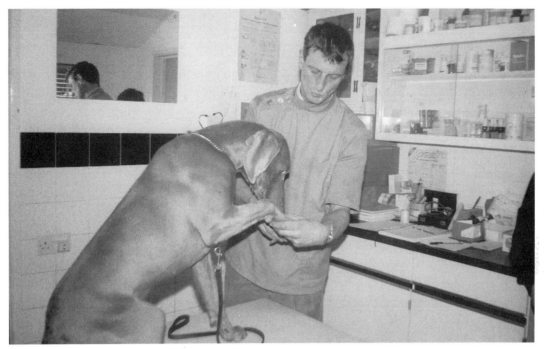

A Weimaraner sits patiently while its nails are trimmed.

damage, as you will be responsible. If your dog is kept in the house it must be taken for walks at regular intervals. If you live in a built-up area the dog must not be allowed to foul other people's gardens or children's play areas. The dog is your responsibility and you must clear up afterwards; poop scoops or plastic bags can easily be purchased and should always be carried when you are exercising your dog.

Keep an eye on your dog's nails and do not let them become too long before cutting them. You can either do the job yourself with nail clippers, or you can take the dog to a vet or grooming parlour. If you attempt to trim the nails, be careful not to cut the quicks as this can be very painful and they will bleed profusely. It is advisable to have some potassium permanganate handy (it is available from all chemists). This will stop the bleeding when it is applied to the nails, but it will also dye your fingers. Some Weimaraners may never need their nails cutting, particularly if they have a lot of road walking, but in my experience dogs seem to carry the genes for short or long nails. When you are cutting the nails, check the feet for any sores or cuts that may need attention.

Your dog will also need to have its ears checked regularly. Weimaraners do not tend to suffer from ear problems because of the absence of hair in their ears; however, you must check that the ear canals are kept clear. If your dog continuously shakes its head these canals can become closed, so it is important that the ears are kept clean and checked for ear mites. I clean ears every six weeks, or more frequently if they appear to. be dirty. To clean the ears, mix a small amount of antiseptic and a small amount of dog shampoo in some warm water – half a cupful is sufficient. Then dip a cotton-wool ball in the mixture, squeeze out the excess moisture, and wipe the inside of the ears and flaps. You will find it easier to do this if the dog is lying on its side, and you can lean on the dog gently to keep it still. Most dogs do not object to this, especially if they have been used to the routine since puppyhood. I have found that the job is simpler if you use a pair of locking forceps. A Weimaraner has large ear canals, so you must be careful not to lose your cotton wool. It can be very dangerous if you probe into the inner ear, so if your dog will not lie still, or you do not feel confident, take it along to the vet, rather than risk causing damage. When you are cleaning, look out for any spots or irritation, and if you find a problem consult your vet. Your Weimaraner's ear flaps or leathers may become dry; this usually affects dogs that get their ears in their dinner, as the food particles dry on them. However, if you apply baby oil twice a week and massage it in well, they will soon become soft again. When you have cleaned your dog's ears, you can check its teeth for any signs of trouble such as loose teeth. If you detect a problem, consult your vet.

BATHING

Weimaraners are low-maintenance dogs because of their short coats. However, all dogs need a bath at least a couple of times a year to keep them fresh and sweet-smelling, and bathing a big lively dog like a Weimaraner can be easier said than done. It conjures up visions of a fight around the bath tub, with very little achieved. However, most Weimaraners can be bathed without any trouble at all, if the following rules are observed.

The dog should be placed in an empty bath, which has a non-slip mat or a folded newspaper in the bottom to stop the dog slipping. Make sure no one else is using the water around the house – such as washing-machines – as this can cause a change of temperature in the water. Mix the shampoo with water in a jug before starting; never use it on the dog straight from the bottle. Then spray the dog gently with warm water, starting with its legs; as it gets used to this you can proceed to its body, starting at the shoulders. Talk to the dog all the time in a gentle, encouraging manner.

When the dog is used to the water, you can then wash its head; this can be done by tipping his nose upwards and spraying from the stop downwards. You can then tip its nose down and wash towards the end of the nose, thus avoiding the eyes. You can apply Vaseline around the eyes before bathing if you are worried about getting water in the eyes. Be careful around the ears, as you do not want to get any water down the ear canals. If the flaps are left hanging they will naturally protect the ears.

Apply your shampoo along the topline, first pouring down each leg. When you get to the head pour a little shampoo in your palm and apply it by hand, making sure it doesn't go in the dog's eyes. Rub in the shampoo – the dog usually enjoys this – and then rinse well. Be careful not to use too strong a shampoo as some Weimaraners have sensitive skins; a mild shampoo applied in moderation will be sufficient. Fortunately this is a breed that is rarely infested by fleas, because of its short coat. If, however, your dog does fall victim, be careful in your choice of shampoo as the strong insecticidal type can cause skin problems. When you have finished rinsing, repeat the whole process, applying shampoo and then rinsing well. If you want to use a conditioner, first mix it in a jug, approximately half water and half conditioner, and apply to the dog in the same way as the shampoo. Leave for a minute and rinse well. I use a standard human hair-conditioner, and I find that this replaces some of the natural oils that have been washed out, and it makes the coat silky and gleaming. When you have rinsed out the conditioner, squeeze out any excess water running down the dog's legs and ear flaps, and stroke its body firmly, which will have the effect of wringing the dog out.

By the time you get to this stage your dog will want to shake. You can avoid this by taking a firm hold of the skin on the back of its neck. A dog always shakes from the neck downwards and this can save mess in the bathroom. Towel the dog down, and then let it go outside for a good shake. When the dog is released, it will probably tear around like a mad thing – I don't know why a bath causes this reaction but it invariably does, so watch out! When the dog is dry, give it a brush and you will end up with a beautiful gleaming, sweet-smelling Weimaraner.

If you show your dog, it must obviously be kept in tip-top condition, and it may require bathing every six to eight weeks, depending on the shows and the weather. Some dogs keep themselves very clean; others, like a bitch I owned, have a penchant for rolling in anything smelly! If you need to bath you dog frequently, make sure you use a very mild shampoo, and always use a conditioner. If you own a long-haired Weimaraner then its coat will need extra care. It will need to be brushed thoroughly at least once a week to ensure that the hair does not become tangled. Coat dressing can be applied to both short-coats and long-coats after bathing, to oil the coat and produce that extra shine.

Weimaraners adapt well to kennel life.

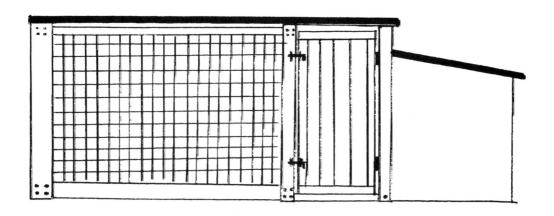

A secure kennel and run.

Chapter Four

BUILDING A KENNEL AND RUN

Why does your dog need a kennel and run? There are some people who are strongly opposed to kennelling, but in my experience I have found that a Weimaraner likes to have its own space, where it can be left in peace and do want it wants. That aside, there are many practical reasons why a kennel is a good idea. There are always occasions, such as weddings, parties, and other functions, when you have to go out and you cannot take your dog with you. In this situation you need somewhere safe and secure where your dog can be kept without getting into any trouble. Secondly, if you work or when you are shopping or having to pick up the children, you can then leave the dog in its kennel, where it cannot do any damage or fall into bad habits. There are also times when you are very busy, and your much-loved dog following you around the house can be surplus to requirements! In this instance, without losing your temper, you can put the dog in its kennel until you have finished being busy, and then the dog can be welcomed back into the house and you can relax in each other's company. If you work your dog, you will often find it is more responsive if it

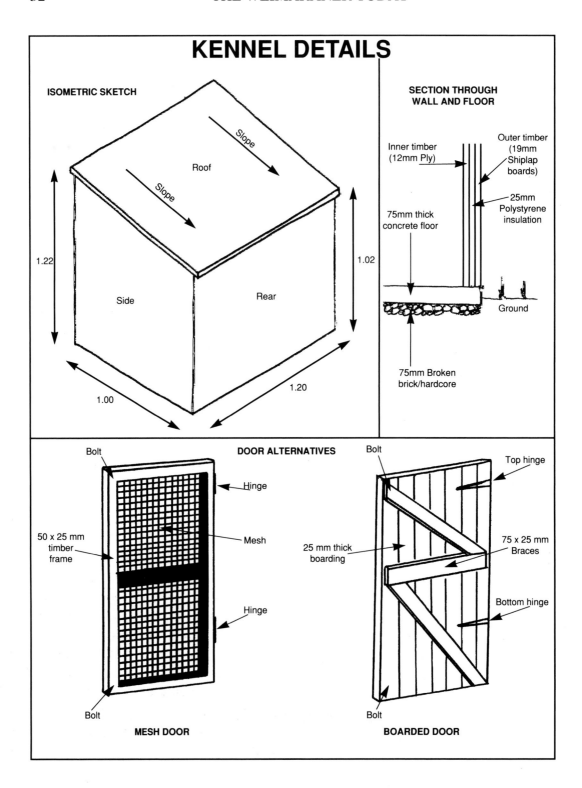

KENNEL DETAILS

ISOMETRIC SKETCH

Slope

Roof

Slope

1.22

1.02

Side

Rear

1.00

1.20

SECTION THROUGH WALL AND FLOOR

Inner timber (12mm Ply)

Outer timber (19mm Shiplap boards)

25mm Polystyrene insulation

75mm thick concrete floor

Ground

75mm Broken brick/hardcore

DOOR ALTERNATIVES

Bolt

Hinge

50 x 25 mm timber frame

Mesh

Hinge

Bolt

MESH DOOR

Bolt

Top hinge

25 mm thick boarding

75 x 25 mm Braces

Bottom hinge

Bolt

BOARDED DOOR

has been kept in a kennel. However, you must remember that a kennel and run is not an exercise area, and your dog will still need a daily walk and a good run, just as it would if it was kept indoors. I also believe that keeping a dog in a kennel and run is preferable to subjecting it to hours of waiting in the car for you. When a dog is in its run it can see the outside world – the birds, next door's cat, and any other happenings.

When you have decided to build a kennel, the next step is to plan what you want and where you want to site it. Choose a position where the kennel will not be in the full sun all day. Dogs like lying out in the sun, but not all day long. If you have limited space and cannot avoid this, you must provide some shade. The kennel can be built against a wall of the house, or garage. This will reduce the cost of the materials, and it will also make one side very secure. Security is all-important in order to stop your dog getting out and other people's dogs getting in. This is particularly vital if you are kennelling a bitch in season.

You can buy kennels and runs ready-made or you can build it all yourself; in both cases you will have to provide a base for the kennel and run. This can be concrete or slabs. If you use slabs, they will have to be grouted in (cement joints) to prevent water and urine seeping through and causing a smell. You must also plan the drainage: waste can go into existing drains or you may need a small soakaway. This can be made quite easily. First you need to dig a hole, then get an old container, five to ten gallons in size, and drill holes in the sides and the base. Place a little shingle in the bottom of the hole, then place the container in the ground, with shingle all round the sides. Finally, place a slab over the top of the container. If you concrete the run floor, make sure the channels in the fall end divert the water to the soakaway. If concrete is used, it must have a smooth finish, as rough concrete can cut a dog's pads.

If you are going to build your own kennel it should be approximately 1m by 1.200m. x 1.020 x 1.220m high. (see diagram). The kennel should be placed outside the run, so the dog cannot jump up on it. I always insulate the kennel sides, roof and floor; this keeps it cool in summer and warm in winter. If you use an old shed, make a hole in the wall (as kennel), and partition part of this off with a removable roof to provide access for cleaning. All the sides should be insulated. The run can be made of any material you have available, but it must have a mesh front and it must be high enough to prevent the dog jumping out or other dogs jumping in. It is preferable if the run has a roof, as this will keep the dog dry when it is raining, and it can also provide shade. Make sure the roof is high enough for you to get inside and clean with ease. The sides can be wood, but make sure it is thick enough to withstand chewing or dogs jumping up against it. Corrugated iron sheets can be used, but if they are secondhand make sure there are no rough nail holes or sharp edges. The size of the run is not important, as long as it is big enough for a fully grown dog to move around in comfort. The size will probably be dictated by the space you have available and how much money you want to spend. Secondhand material such as wood, slabs, mesh and sheets of tin can be obtained from demolition companies. Concrete can be made from all-in (sand and shingle) mixed with cement. The proportions are: minimum 8 of all-in to 1 cement, maximum 5 all-in to 1 cement. The minimum thickness of the concrete is 075m (3ins). Make sure that there are no weeds or grass under the concrete and the site has a fall to the soakaway. Put the corner posts in concrete before concreting the run, and treat the wood with non-toxic preservative.

For the kennel insulation I use polystyrene, which can be bought in 8 x 4 ft. sheets, or you can go to a local builder for off-cuts. This must be fitted in between the inner and outer walls of the kennel. The door can be made of mesh or wood, as long as it is secure. If you use mesh, you will have to make a frame, and brace the middle. The ideal is .075m x .050m timber. If you are using wood, it must be .025m (1 inch) thick board to the width, then to the cross pieces, and a brace from one side cross piece to the other cross piece. The door must be hinged top and bottom, and bolted top and bottom. This will stop the door springing when the dog jumps on it, and stops the dog trapping itself.

When the kennel is ready, introduce your dog to it slowly and carefully, encouraging it as you would with any new experience. In time, your dog will accept its second home, and you will be secure in the knowledge that you have a safe place to leave your dog. A kennel does not mean that a dog is confined day and night, but it gives you the flexibility to choose when you want your dog in the house, which will ultimately lead to a better relationship between you and your dog.

Chapter Five

THE BREED STANDARD

THE BRITISH BREED STANDARD

GENERAL APPEARANCE Medium-sized, grey with light eyes. Presents a picture of power, stamina and balance.

CHARACTERISTICS Hunting ability of paramount concern.

TEMPERAMENT Fearless, friendly, protective, obedient and alert.

HEAD AND SKULL Moderately long, aristocratic; moderate stop, slight median line extending back over forehead. Rather prominent occipital bone. Measurement from top of nose to stop equal to measurement from stop to occipital prominence. Flews moderately deep, enclosing powerful jaw. Foreface straight, and delicate at the nostrils. Skin tightly drawn. Nose grey.

Sh. Ch. Czersieger Clever Clown: This male is powerfully built and shows good length of body.
Owned by Colin Hill. Bred by Mrs Sieglinde Smith.   *Dalton.*

EYES Medium-sized, shades of amber or blue-grey. Placed far enough apart to indicate good disposition, not too protruding or deeply set. Expression keen, kind and intelligent.

EARS Long, lobular, slightly folded, set high. When drawn alongside jaw, should end approximately 2.5cms (1 inch) from point of nose.

MOUTH Jaws strong with a perfect, regular and complete scissor bite, i.e. upper teeth closely overlapping lower teeth and set square to the jaws. Lips and gums of pinkish, flesh colour. Complete dentition highly desirable.

NECK Clean cut and moderately long.

FOREQUARTERS Forelegs straight and strong. Measurement from elbow to ground equal to distance from elbow to top of withers.

BODY Length of body from highest point of withers to root of tail should equal the

Sh. Ch. Gunalt Anais Anais: Junior Warrant and winner of 29 CCs. This bitch conforms beautifully to the Breed Standard. She has a nice neck and shoulders, good all-round conformation and sound in movement.
Owned and bred by Mr and Mrs S. A. Hollings.   *Dave Freeman*

measurement from the highest point of withers to ground. Topline level, with slightly sloping croup. Chest well developed, deep. Shoulders well laid. Ribs well sprung, ribcage extending well back. Abdomen firmly held, moderately tucked up flank. Brisket should drop to elbow.

HINDQUARTERS Moderately angulated with well turned stifle. Hocks well let down, turned neither in nor out. Musculation well developed.

FEET Firm, compact. Toes well arched, pads close, thick. Nails short, grey or amber in colour. Dew claws customarily removed.

TAIL Customarily docked so that remaining tail covers scrotum in dogs and vulva in bitches. Thickness of tail in proportion to body, and should be carried in a manner expressing confidence and sound temperament. In long-haired tip of tail may be removed.

GAIT/MOVEMENT Effortless, ground covering, indicating smooth co-ordination, Seen from rear, hindfeet parallel to front feet. Seen from side, topline remains strong and level.

COAT Short, smooth and sleek. In long-haired variety, coat from 2.5-5cms (1-2 inches) long on body, somewhat longer on neck, chest and belly. Tail and back of limbs, feathered.

COLOUR Preferably silver grey, shades of mouse or roe grey permissible; blending to lighter shade on head and ears. Dark eel stripe frequently occurs along back. Whole coat gives an appearance of metallic sheen. Small white mark permissible on chest. White spots resulting from injuries not penalised.

SIZE Height at withers; Dogs 61-69cms (24-27ins); bitches 56-64cms (22-25ins).

FAULTS Any departure from the foregoing points should be considered a fault and the seriousness with which the fault should be regarded should be in exact proportion to its degree.

NOTE Male animals should have two apparently normal testicles fully descended into the scrotum.
Reproduced by kind permission of the English Kennel Club.

THE AMERICAN BREED STANDARD

GENERAL APPEARANCE A medium-sized gray dog, with fine aristocratic features. He should present a picture of grace, speed, stamina, alertness and balance. Above all, the dog's conformation must indicate the ability to work with great speed and endurance in the field.

HEIGHT Height at the withers: dogs, 25 to 27 inches; bitches. 23 to 25 inches. One inch over or under the specified height of each sex is allowable but should be penalized. Dogs measuring less than 24 inches or more than 28 inches and bitches measuring less than 22 inches or more then 26 inches shall be disqualified.

HEAD Moderately long and aristocratic, with moderate stop and slight median line extending back over the forehead. Rather prominent occipital bone and trumpets well set back, beginning at the back of the eye sockets. Measurement from tip of nose to stop equal that from stop to occipital bone. The flews should be straight, delicate at the nostrils. Skin drawn tightly. Neck clean-cut and moderately long. Expression kind, keen and intelligent.

EARS Long and lobular, slightly folded and set high. The ear when drawn snugly alongside the jaw should end approximately 2 inches from the point of the nose.

EYES In shades of light amber, gray or blue-gray, set well enough apart to indicate good disposition and intelligence. When dilated under excitement the eyes may appear almost black.

TEETH Well set, strong and even; well-developed and proportionate to jaw with correct scissors bite, the upper teeth protruding slightly over the lower teeth but not more than $\frac{1}{16}$ of an inch. Complete dentition is greatly to be desired.

NOSE Gray.

LIPS AND GUMS Pinkish flesh shades.

BODY The back should be moderate in length, set in a straight line, strong, and should slope slightly from the withers. The chest should be well developed and deep with shoulders well laid back. Ribs well sprung and long. Abdomen firmly held; moderately tucked-up flank. The brisket should extend to the elbow.

COAT AND COLOR Short, smooth and sleek, solid color, in shades of mouse-gray to silver-gray, usually blending to lighter shades on the head and ears. A small white marking on the chest is permitted, but should be penalized on any other portion of the body. White spots resulting from injury should not be penalized. A distinctly long coat is a disqualification. A distinctly blue or black coat is a disqualification.

FORELEGS Straight and strong, with the measurement from the elbow to the ground approximately equaling the distance from the elbow to the top of the withers.

HINDQUARTERS Well-angulated stifles and straight hocks. Musculation well developed.

FEET Firm and compact, webbed, toes well arched, pads closed and thick, nails short and gray or amber in color. Dewclaws should be removed.

TAIL Docked. At maturity it should measure approximately 6 inches with a tendency to be light rather than heavy and should be carried in a manner expressing confidence and sound temperament. A non-docked tail shall be penalized.

GAIT The gait should be effortless and should indicate smooth coordination. When seen from the rear, the hind feet should be parallel to the front feet. When viewed from the side, the topline should remain strong and level.

TEMPERAMENT Should be friendly, fearless, alert and obedient.

FAULTS

Minor Faults: Tail too short or too long. Pink nose.

Major Faults: Doggy bitches. Bitchy dogs. Improper muscular condition. Badly affected teeth. More than four teeth missing. Back too long or too short. Faulty coat. Neck too short, thick or throaty. Low-set tail. Elbows in or out. Feet east and west. Poor gait. Poor feet. Cow hocks. Faulty backs, either roached or sway. Badly overshot, or undershot bite. Snipy muzzle. Short ears.

Very Serious Faults: White, other than a spot on the chest. Eyes other than gray, blue-gray or light amber. Black mottled mouth. Non-docked tail. Dogs exhibiting strong fear, shyness or extreme nervousness.

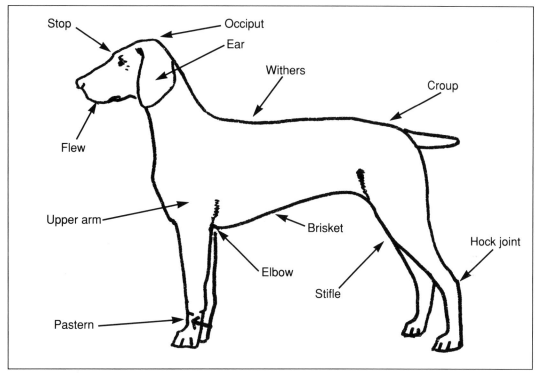

Points of a Weimaraner with good length and medium-sized.

DISQUALIFICATIONS

Deviation in height of more than one inch from Standard either way. A distinctly long coat. A distinctly blue or black coat.

Reproduced by kind permission of the American Kennel Club.

ANALYSIS OF THE BREED STANDARD

The Breed Standard is a blueprint of the perfect dog. This elusive perfect specimen has never been produced, so every dog you see has varying faults or varying points that could be improved upon. When you read the Breed Standard you should look at the whole of the Standard, and not just focus on some points, as this can lead to an unbalanced view. For instance, you might penalise a dog with short ears, but turn a blind eye to a dog whose ears are too long. The aim is for your dog to fit the Breed Standard, rather than trying to make the Breed Standard fit your dog. All dogs have

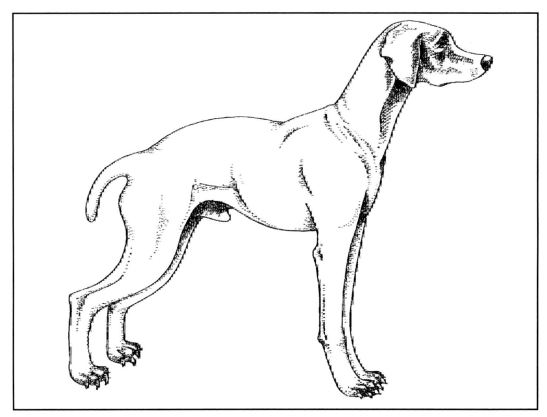

Incorrect: too short in back, snipy nose, dished head, lack of flew, short ears, weak pasterns, roachy back, poor tail carriage, sickle hocks.

faults, so be realistic about your dog's shortcomings; this will ultimately help you to handle your dog to advantage in the show ring.

GENERAL APPEARANCE This covers the overall appearance of the dog – from movement to muscle condition. The overall picture should give the impression of power and strength, without any coarseness. The dog or bitch should have good bone, and should not appear too fine or gangly. It should look well muscled and look as if it is capable of doing a day's work in the field. The American Weimaraner tends to look slightly more angulated than the British specimen. The dog and bitch should both have a distinctive head: the dog must not look too 'bitchy' and the bitch should look feminine with a lighter head, but she must still have good bone. The Weimaraner is a medium-sized breed, and so dogs should not be too tall. Tall dogs tend to be very straight either in shoulder placement or rear angulation, and this can give a stilted action when the dog is moving, due to the lack of extension at both

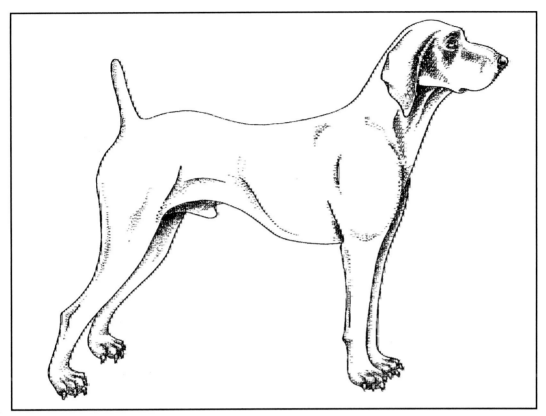

Incorrect: too long in back, throaty (too much skin), Roman nose, gay tail, sway back, loaded shoulder, lack of rear angulation in stifle joint.

fore and rear end. Ideally, the Weimaraner should be silver-grey in colour, which is the hallmark of the breed.

CHARACTERISTICS AND TEMPERAMENT This comes down to a personal assessment of how you see the dog in question, but hopefully something of the dog's personality will come across in the show ring. The Weimaraner should be friendly and outgoing, it should never be nervous, and most show a liking for children. However, this is a proud breed, and rival males can be competitive. All Weimaraners are very intelligent and will learn quickly – good and bad habits – so it is important that they are treated firmly and with kindness in order to maintain mutual respect. In this way, the Weimaraner will become a devoted companion, and most people who have owned a Weimaraner never want any other breed of dog.

HEAD AND SKULL Eyes and ears can be seen by different people in different

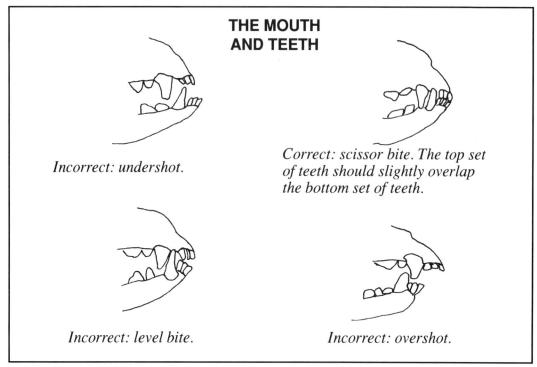

**THE MOUTH
AND TEETH**

Incorrect: undershot.

Correct: scissor bite. The top set of teeth should slightly overlap the bottom set of teeth.

Incorrect: level bite.

Incorrect: overshot.

ways – beauty is in the eye of the beholder. However, the measurements should be adhered to. Dogs should have a stronger head than bitches, and a head that is too broad or too narrow should be penalised in both sexes. Weimaraners in the show ring today are showing a tendency to be snipy and to be losing the flews – the pendulous upper lip. There are also some specimens which are very heavy in the head and broad-skulled, and these give an appearance which is more akin to a Bull Mastiff than an elegant Weimaraner.

The nose should not turn up like a Pointer, but it should be level from the stop to the nose. The flews should be long and cover the bottom jaw. The eye-set on a dog can alter its whole expression. In the case of the Weimaraner the eyes should not be set too close together or too far apart, and they should not give a staring appearance. The eye should be kind and soft, giving the dog a gentle expression. The Weimaraner should not appear red-eyed or runny, and the rims should not be baggy. The colour of the eye-rims and nose should match the colour of the coat.

MOUTH A complete scissor bite is essential. If the dog does not have a good bite it may have problems biting and chewing its food. Bad mouths are usually hereditary and there is little that can be done to improve them. Dogs with this defect should be penalised as they do not make suitable breeding stock.

Anstar Pinot Noir shows a nice aristocratic head on a male – it is without any sign
of coarseness.   *Owned and bred by Mr and Mrs J. Saker.*

NECK Clean-cut means no throatiness, i.e. no loose skin hanging down from the throat. In severe cases this can give the dog the appearance of a Bloodhound. The neck should be moderately long, and it should fit the shoulders neatly. It should not give the impression of a yew-necked horse and look as though it is fitted on upside

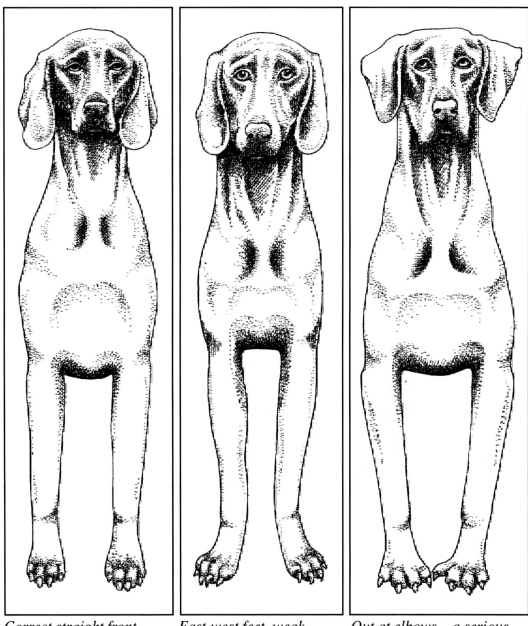

Correct straight front.

East-west feet, weak pasterns, lack of forechest.

Out at elbows – a serious fault in bone structure – and pigeon-toed.

down! The skin should fit neatly around the muscles to give an appearance of strength.

FOREQUARTERS Forelegs must be straight, and any variations from this should

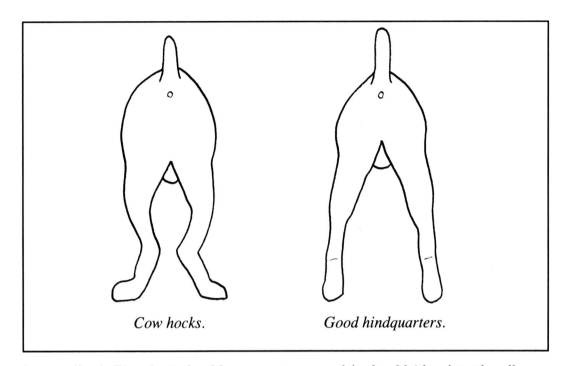

Cow hocks.   *Good hindquarters.*

be penalised. The chest should appear strong and it should 'drop' to the elbows. There seems to be a lot of space between the chest and the elbows on some exhibits today, and this highlights the lack of substance required in a Weimaraner. There should be ample space between the forelegs, without the dog appearing too wide. Elbows should never stick out, as this is a serious fault in bone construction. A dog with this problem can never move straight and true, as required with this breed. From a rear angle this can be seen better, especially when the dog is on the move. A dog with this problem should not be used in any breeding programme.

BODY The body measurements should give the appearance of being longer than tall, but only by virtue of the head and tail. The Weimaraner should never look short in body, as this gives the impression of being short and stocky in length, and this alters the whole look of the breed. Toplines should be level, never roached, and they should remain level on the move.

HINDQUARTERS These are the power behind a dog, and a Weimaraner should drive from the rear. Unfortunately, many Weimaraners appear to have lost this action, and tend to drive from the front. A dog that is moving correctly, driving off from the rear, will put little effort into its movement. Its stride will be long, and it will need a fair amount of space to show its true movement, as its ground coverage

Sh. Ch. Trilite Tegans Girl of Hagar: Winner of the Gundog Group at Windsor Championship Show, Weimaraner Club of Great Britain's Weimaraner of the Year in 1989 and Top Show Dog (All Breeds) in Scotland 1989. This bitch has a beautiful pale silver coat which is typical of the Weimaraner.
Owned by Dennis White. Bred by Tony Rainey.

is considerable. Its front movement will be very light. When a dog is driving off the front, it will look as though it is putting a lot of effort into its stride, but it will not be covering much ground. Its stride will be short in length, and it would tire easily if it was worked.

TAIL As with most breeds, docking is optional in Britain, but most judges will penalise long tails to a degree depending on other virtues. Tails should be carried level with the topline, never 'gay' or up on end. A low tail carriage or a tail held down usually denotes an unhappy dog or in some cases it can point to temperamental problems. In America a non-docked tail is listed as a very serious fault. However, in Scandinavia tail-docking is now illegal.

GAIT AND MOVEMENT This should be effortless, with good ground covering i.e. front legs reaching for the ground and good extension of rear legs. If the dog is too straight in the shoulder and stifle, the movement will be stilted and the dog will be very active in movement, but very short in strides.

COAT AND COLOUR This has provoked much debate in recent years. The Breed Standard states "Preferably silver-grey, shades of mouse or roe grey permissible", so by this I think silver-grey is the desired colour but other virtues can be taken into consideration e.g. a good roe grey is better than a bad silver-grey. If the colour is any darker I do not think the dog should be bred from or placed at a show. In America a black or blue-coloured Weimaraner would be disqualified, but this is not the case in Britain. Small white marking is permissible on the chest, but this should be kept to a minimum. The long-coated Weimaraner is part of the English Breed Standard, and some Championship Shows and Breed Club Shows have classes scheduled specially for them. However, the coat must be no more than one to two inches in length. In America dogs with a distinctly long coat are disqualified.

SIZE I believe that one inch either way is acceptable, but the middle of the height standard should be the norm. The American Breed Standard stipulates a minimum size in males of 25ins and in females 23ins – one inch taller than the English Standard, and dogs are disqualified if they deviate more than one inch either way from the height Standard. In Britain some dogs are placed even if they are well over the required height. There are very few small Weimaraners as the breed appears to be getting bigger in recent years. Both the American and the English Breed Standards agree that the drop of brisket should fall to the elbow. This gives the Weimaraner plenty of heart-room, which enables it to work with ease.

Any departure from the Breed Standard is a fault, but every dog has faults and virtues, so these should be balanced against each other and determined by their degree. Try to form your interpretation of the Breed Standard by studying dogs from different kennels and breeders – not just in the ring, but also when the dogs are relaxed. In time, you will see that each kennel has its own hallmarks, most often seen in the head properties. Every person has different ideas as to which dogs are best, and every kennel or breeder thinks they have the best, so it is up to you to decide which type of dog suits you.

Hasswyn Stainsby Girl aged three weeks.

Chapter Six

THE LONG-HAIRED WEIMARANER

"What did you cross your Weimaraner with?" "How did you keep the tail on your dog?" "Is that really a long-haired Weimaraner?" These are just some of the comments you get if you own one of these beautiful members of our breed. The long-haired variety has been in Britain for some eighteen years, but their progress towards becoming an established and recognised part of the breed has been both erratic and slow.

The first long-haired Weimaraner to be born in Britain was Mafia Man of Monroes, who was produced by two short-haired parents in 1973. In the same year a long-haired bitch, Asta Von gut Blastanden, was imported by Roy and Ann Janson, followed in 1974 by the male, Dino Von Der Hagardburg, also imported by Roy and Ann Janson. A third male, Hasso Von Der Hagardburg, was imported in 1979 by Mr and Mrs L. Smith. Since this time, the majority of long-haired dogs in Britain have been sired by or originate back to these dogs. A small percentage of long-hairs were the result of matings with short-haired Weimaraners. These mixed matings were part

Damaris Twilight (left), Weimaraner of the Year in 1987, with Hawsvale Whitebeam and Coppetwood Domino Marcaste.

of a plan to try and eliminate the problem of epilepsy by expanding the gene pool. The bloodlines of the long-haired became very close, and quite recently some long-hairs have been found to be suffering from epilepsy. However, there have been further matings to short-haired stock carrying the long-haired gene, and these appear in the main to have been successful both in improving the overall standard of the long-haired and in helping to minimise the recurrence of past problems. These matings must be carefully planned on both sides – long-hairs and short-hairs – as neither party wants to pass on any inherent problems. It would, I think, be fair to say that the standard of short-coat offspring from these matings has not been detrimental to the breed.

There is also the question of tail docking, as it is difficult to differentiate between the two coats at an early age. It is therefore necessary to find a vet that is sympathetic to your aims, who will be prepared to dock at a later date, under an anaesthetic. This may become increasingly difficult as more vets move towards anti-docking, but if legislation was to ban docking altogether, it would cease to be a problem, as even the short-hairs would have a full tail. Hopefully, these mixed matings can be built upon, and perhaps, with the arrival of more imports, further

Vimana El Supremo: The long-coat should conform to exactly the same Breed Standard as the short-coat. In most cases it is just the tip of the tail that is docked.

improvements can be made. Despite the relatively small numbers, the long-hairs are great ambassadors for the breed, gaining much admiration and comment from the non-Weimaraner-owning dog world.

Numerically, few long-hairs competed for honours in the show ring, but there are those that have enjoyed considerable success. Aruni Dinwiddi from Seicer, bred and owned by Mr and Mrs Janson, won two Challenge Certificates and two Reserve Challenge Certificates, and was the first long-hair to win a ticket. Pondridge Practical Joker followed in Didi's footsteps, and in July 1991 he made breed history by becoming the first long-haired Weimaraner to be made a Show Champion. He is owned by Shirley Anderton and was bred by Mr and Mrs L. Smith. Pondridge Anna Adele, also bred by Mr and Mrs Smith and owned by Mrs V. Blyth, is the only long-haired bitch to have won a Challenge Certificate, to date. A number of young long-hairs are currently doing well in the show ring. They are: Phantom Piper of Pondridge and Pondridge Paper Moon, owned by Mr and Mrs L. Smith; Coppitwood Domino Marcasite owned by Mrs Ruth Williams; and Vimana El Supremo owned by Mr and Mrs Robinson. Perhaps one of these dogs may be the first long-haired Show Champion? The long-hairs also have brains as well as beauty: they make good working gundogs, and their typical Weimaraner stubbornness, together with their willingness to please, makes an interesting and challenging training combination. The long-hairs seem to take to water more readily, and they face thicker cover better than their short-coat relatives – probably because they have their coat to protect them and keep them warm! Successes in field competitions have been few but significant: Hawsvale Whitebeam, owned by Mrs Ruth Williams, was the first long-haired bitch to win a Certificate of Merit; and Wyndlee Silver Candy, owned by Dorothy Shall, has won three Certificates of Merit, and a third place – all at Novice Field Trials. Wyndlee Silver Candy has also won the *Shooting Times* Challenge Trophy for three consecutive years, and has won awards both for Best Field Trial dog and for Weimaraner of the Year of the South East Branch of the Weimaraner Club of Great Britain.

Long-hairs have enjoyed greater success in Working Trials. Damaris Twilight, owned by Mrs Ruth Williams, has gained the qualifications CD ex, UD ex, WD ex and TD ex, and helped by these achievements she also won The Weimaraner Club of Great Britain Bruno Trophy for Working Trials, and the Weimaraner of the Year award in 1987. Her daughter Coppetwood Domino Marcasite, also owned and bred by Ruth Williams, is following in her mother's footsteps, and is consistently well placed in Working Trials. She was sired by Champion Reeman Aruac CD ex, UD ex, WD ex, TD ex, owned by Mr R. Lynch.

Overseas the long-hairs enjoy mixed popularity. In their native Germany, approximately 15 per cent of the Weimaraner population is long-haired. However, in neighbouring Austria, the majority of Weimaraners are long-haired, though the breed itself is small in numbers. There is a fairly high proportion of breeders of long-hairs in Czechoslovakia, where the wire-haired Weimaraner is also recognised. There are long-hairs in Australia and New Zealand in small numbers, and in Australia a litter has recently been born using frozen semen from Britain. There are also a number of long-hairs in South Africa, and a small number in France, Holland and Italy. In America the long-haired variety is not recognised, and a long coat on a Weimaraner is considered a serious fault.

Occasionally, long-hairs appear in American breeding, courtesy of two short-haired parents, and these are highly prized by the small band of long-haired enthusiasts. Despite the very small number of long-hairs in the States, they achieve a high level of success in Field Trials and obedience tests. In Holland the long-hairs compete very favourably, both at show and in field trials, against the short-hairs, and in Germany and Austria the long-hairs have taken many top field and working trial awards. In Austria, probably owing to their proportionately greater numbers, the long-hairs have achieved success in Best of Breed and Group awards under FCI

The long-coated Weimaraner shows the same aptitude in Working Trials and Field Trials as the short-coat.

rules, where they are shown separately from short-hairs.

There is no doubt that the long-haired Weimaraner has much to contribute to the breed – in the show ring, in the Field and in Working Trials. Breeders must concentrate on building a sound foundation for this variety, which can be developed and expanded in future years. The Breed Standard for both varieties is identical, with the exception of the length of coat, so the aim of all enthusiasts should be to breed sound and typical Weimaraners – with the correct length of coat.

Handler Andrew Westwood training a five-month-old puppy for the show ring.

Chapter Seven

TRAINING FOR
THE SHOW RING

If you embark on show training your Weimaraner, you must be fully aware of what is required of you and your dog in the ring. You must understand the Kennel Club rules and regulations and learn about ring etiquette. Kennel Club rules govern all dog shows and a copy of them can be obtained from the Kennel Club at a modest price. If you break these rules you may face a fine or even have your dog disqualified from showing, so take time to study them carefully.

The best way of learning about showing dogs is to attend a show. If you have watched other people handling their dogs, and are familiar with procedures in the ring, you will get off to a good start when you take the plunge. You must also try to assess the dog that you are planning to show. You probably think your dog is the best specimen ever to appear on the Weimaraner scene, but remember, all the competitors will think they have best dog. Your job is to convince the judges that your dog deserves the honours, and the better it is presented, the better it will do. The aim is to catch the judge's eye, but this should be achieved by skilful handling –

not wearing something flamboyant! Obviously you will not win every time you show your dog, but remember, your dog did not ask to compete. You must always praise your dog for its efforts, no matter the result, and be confident that the best dog is always the one you take home at the end of the day. Try to look at your dog objectively; study it and get to know its faults. If you need expert advice, go back to your dog's breeder to get a balanced assessment. Your dog must conform to the Breed Standard in all its most important points; if it doesn't, there is no point in going in for competition. Learn the Breed Standard, and when you have assessed your dog against it, don't go around asking lots of different people what they think of your dog; you will only become confused as everyone sees different things in different dogs. If you have made up your mind you want to show your dog and you are confident that it conforms with the Breed Standard, then don't let anyone try to change your mind.

If you are a newcomer to showing, it is a good idea to join a local training club which specialises in show-training. This will give you the opportunity to meet other novices and gain experience from people who have shown regularly. You will still have to do a lot of training at home, and you may find it a lot easier to work your dog in a situation that has fewer distractions. Training classes are very good for socializing your dog, but do find out which dogs are friendly and which are not. Go the first time without your dog, and then you will find out which dogs to avoid. There is nothing worse than taking your lovely friendly puppy along to a class, and then, without warning, it is snapped at by an aggressive dog. All training that you undertake with your dog must be gradual; you will have to be patient and firm.

One of the first lessons is to teach your dog to stand still. This is an unnatural pose for a dog, and to begin with it will probably fidget. Don't worry about this, or any other problem in the initial stages of training, you will not gain anything. Stay calm and be patient, and you will get there in the end. Ring training should commence as soon as the puppy is walking well on the lead. It should be regarded an extension of ordinary training, and not treated as something different. By this stage, your puppy should be quite happy on its lead, and it should be familiar with noise and traffic. I use a slip lead, and to start with I take the puppy for a walk, to settle it. This does not mean walking for miles – a puppy should never be over-exercised. If you watch a puppy at home, it will alternate periods of activity with periods of rest. However, when you go out for a walk the puppy will follow you, and it can become over-tired if you walk too far. Excessive road-work can have a damaging effect on the bone structure of puppies, so remember that your puppy is still growing and all road-work must be moderated. When you have returned from your short walk you can then proceed with five minutes lead work. Talk to your puppy and encourage it to walk in a straight line, then turn, and come back in a straight line to where you started. You will probably find that the puppy is all over the place to start with, but if you talk to it quietly and firmly, it will soon get the message.

When you have completed this procedure, try to get your puppy to stand. To begin with, the aim is to get the puppy to stand still. Command your puppy saying "stand", and hold it gently under the head. Never use force on the puppy; if it fidgets, break the exercise by turning the puppy around your legs, and try again. Puppies cannot concentrate for long periods of time – five minutes is long enough to start with – so don't expect too much too soon. When your puppy has learnt to stand still, you can then start placing its feet. In the show ring a Weimaraner must stand square; the front legs must be straight and the feet must point forwards. The rear legs must not be placed too far back, which would upset the natural balance of the dog, the back feet must point forwards, and the hocks should be straight. Start off by placing the front legs. This can be done either by picking up the dog's front end and placing it square on the ground, or by placing each leg. Look at the dog's front when it is placed and check that it is square. When you are training a youngster you will probably find that the minute you get the front right and start placing the back, the dog moves. This can be frustrating, but you just start again, talking to your dog and encouraging it.

It is important not to let go of the dog's head when you are trying to place the feet. This sounds as though you need to have three arms, but there is a relatively straightforward way of doing it! Hold the dog's head gently under the jaw with one hand and then place each front leg, in turn, with the other hand, instructing the dog to "stand" in a firm voice. Then, still holding the dog's head, place the back feet. The reason for holding the dog's head is to ensure that it maintains concentration throughout the duration of the exercise. Weimaraners are very easy to train, but they can be stubborn on occasions. When this happens, never use force; gentle handling will always produce the best results. As soon as the puppy has stood still – even if it only for five minutes – praise it lavishly. Then break the exercise by turning the puppy around you, and walk briskly in a straight line, turn and walk back. The dog should follow quite happily as it will think it is going for a walk. Talk to it and encourage it all the time, using its name and plenty of praise. As the dog gets better at walking in a straight line, you can then speed up to a trot. The aim is to get the dog moving fluently at a gentle pace, progressing in a straight line. When the dog has settled into a nice, easy gait, turn it and bring it back to the starting point. If the dog becomes unsettled in its movement, return to a walk, and continue at this speed until the dog has settled again. When you have mastered moving in a straight line you can attempt the triangle. This involves keeping the dog straight to each corner, and then returning to the starting point and finishing with the dog standing square. By this stage you will have graduated to fifteen minute training sessions, including running out and standing. Practice makes perfect, but it is equally important to remember that if you work a dog for too long in the initial stages it will become bored, and a bored dog will never show well. Three training sessions a week is sufficient for a five-month-old puppy; these should be short in length, and they should appear to be fun, so the dog enjoys them.

When you have mastered the basics at home you will be ready to go to show training classes, and amongst other things, your puppy will have to get used to having its mouth inspected. You can practise this at home, gently opening its mouth and giving lots of praise. At the class someone will 'go over' your puppy, which means someone running their hands over the dog's body to feel any faults. The judge will do this at a show, so the dog must get used to it. Most dogs love being handled, and they usually enjoy going to classes. Weimaraners love attention, and most will be only too happy to reward you by doing what is required.

Chapter Eight

SHOWING YOUR DOG

When you have trained your dog for the show ring, you will probably be itching to get going and try your first competition. However, with a puppy you must be patient, and do not attempt to do too much. If you over-show a puppy it may become bored and, in time, it may decide that it does not like dog shows, and it will make this only too apparent in the ring. In Britain, puppies cannot be shown under the age of six months and must not be on the precincts of the show ground under that age. When your puppy is over six months you can enter your dog as 'Not for Competition', which will enable you to take the puppy for a look around, before you enter serious competition. Most shows are usually advertised approximately eight weeks in advance, so if you are contemplating showing your puppy at six months you will have to start looking in the dog Press when your puppy is four months of age. The usual procedure is to apply to the secretary of the show you wish to attend, and then you receive a schedule. This will include a copy of the rules and regulations of the society holding the show, and the Kennel Club rules. When you sign the entry form, it means that you will abide by these rules. All the scheduled classes for your breed will be explained so you know which class to enter. In Britain if you are showing a

Ragstone Weimaraners: Ringtaube, Russelle and Ryotsquad. This kennel has produced many winners in the show ring.

puppy that is under nine months of age then you can enter it for 'Minor Puppy'. There is not always a class for this, so you may have to enter 'Puppy', which is for dogs under twelve months. The age stipulation relates to the age of the puppy on the first day of the show. If there isn't a puppy class you will have to enter 'Junior'. However, if you are placed and not beaten by another puppy, you will still be Best Puppy in Breed. It sounds very complicated, but if you are confused either making your entry, or on the day, don't be afraid to ask the show secretary. Send in your entry before the closing date on the form, with your cheque. If you are making several entries for shows write down the closing dates and the show dates in your diary. Special show diaries can be purchased from show stands and through dog papers, and they will have the principal show dates marked. After I have posted my entries I usually write 'Gone' in the diary, and also the name of the dog I have entered. If you have several dogs it is surprisingly easy to forget which dog you have entered, and this will save you the embarrassment of having to telephone the show secretary to find out!

Vicky Bambridge poses Beckstone Special Edition J.W.: Winner of sixty firsts at Championship and Open Shows.

Mr and Mrs J. Saker are known for their Anstar Weimaraners. Pictured left to right: Wave of Sylt, Dangford Renidia, Anstar Perfidia and Anstar Pinot Noir.

There are a number of different kinds of shows you can enter in Britain, ranging from one-day shows to larger four-day Championship shows.

EXEMPTION SHOWS

These are one-day shows, and entries are not accepted before the day of the show – all you have to do is turn up on the day of the show. Dogs do not need not be registered with the Kennel Club, and all breeds can enter – including mongrels. The purpose of Exemption shows is to raise money for a worthwhile cause, and they provide a fun day out for the family.

LIMIT SHOWS

These are limited to members only, but you can join the society concerned when making your entry. Dogs that are Champions and dogs that have won a Challenge Certificate are not allowed to compete.

Sh. Ch. Hansom Hospitality: Winner of 3 CCs and 2 RCCs, and Best Gundog in Show at a Guernsey Show.
Owned by J. Kneebone. Bred by Mr. R. M. W. Finch.   *Pearce.*

OPEN SHOWS
These are open to everyone with a registered pedigree dog, whether you are a member of the organising body or not. Entries must be prepaid and sent in with your entry form to the secretary. Wet weather accommodation is provided.

CHAMPIONSHIP SHOWS
This can be a one-day breed Championship show, or a general Championship show, which can run over three or four days. These are the only shows where your dog can qualify for Crufts. Large numbers of dogs and people attend Championship

shows, and strict rules apply. All entries must be sent in advance, and this will sometimes include a charge for car parking and a catalogue. Before the date of the show, you will receive passes for the show, which will give your dog entry to the show. You must not forget these on the day, and you may be asked to show your passes if you want to leave the show ground at any time, so don't throw them away after you have first gained admission. When you and your dog are in the show ground the next step is to collect your catalogue and look under your breed for your name and number – and the number in the catalogue will be your bench number. Sometimes these numbers are posted to you in advance. Then make your way to the benching area allocated to your breed, which is usually well sign-posted. Be careful when you are walking between the benches with your dog, as not all dogs are friendly. You must come provided with a blanket, collar and benching chain, and when you get to your bench you can settle your dog on its blanket and secure it with its benching chain. You can place your show bag, with all your equipment under the bench.

Make sure you arrive at the show in plenty of time; judging times are usually printed in the show schedule – any changes will be printed in the dog papers. You must allow for travelling time – heavy traffic and road closures are added difficulties. It is better to arrive an hour early than ten minutes late. After locating your bench, check to see if there are two cards on the top: take one, as this is your ring number. If there is only one card, it means that numbers will be collected in the ring. You must then go and locate your ring, which is usually near the benching area, and you can see what is going on. It is important you get to the ring-side for your class when judging commences – they will not wait for you. Before your class is due to start it is wise to work your dog for five or ten minutes to give it a chance to settle and relax. Wait until your class is called by the steward, and then, if you have not already got it, you will collect your number card from the steward in the ring, and this must be clipped on.

The dog classes are judged first and when these have been judged the Challenge Certificate or CC, also known as a 'ticket', will be awarded to the best dog, and the Reserve CC goes to the second best dog. The same procedure is then followed for the bitches, and then the two sexes meet for the Best of Breed to be awarded. The winner will then represent the breed in the Gundog Group. A Best Puppy is usually awarded in each breed, and again, this will be decided between the best dog and the best bitch puppies. There is not always an award for the Best Puppy in Show.

When judging is over you can return to your bench and give your dog a drink, and give it a chance to rest on its bench. Remember, your dog is your responsibility even when it is benched, and it must not be a nuisance to other people or other dogs, and

Sh. Ch. Warehead Marion of Rangatira.   Owned by Mr and Mrs C. Brown.

it is not wise to leave it alone for long periods of time. Championship shows usually have restricted arrival and departure times, so that there is plenty going on throughout the day for the paying visitors to see. Some Championship shows will allow you to leave early when the weather is hot; however, I prefer to leave later in the day when the temperature falls.

If you are going to show your dog on a regular basis, you will need to be organised and pack a show bag with all the items you will require. I always take:

A benching chain.
Collar.
An unbreakable dog's bowl for water.
A small plastic bottle containing water.
Hand wipes (it's surprising how dirty your hands get at shows
  – don't forget you have to eat your dinner).
A tube of anti-sting cream, for insect bites and stings
  – you can use this on either you or your dog.

Sh. Ch. Fineshade Magical Mystery: Winner of 6 CCs.
Owned by Mr. G. Shaw. Bred by Mrs J. George.

Show passes and schedule (check these the night before the show
to save a mad panic in the morning).
Waterproof coat.
Road map.
Pedal-bin liners (ideal for clearing up after your dog, should it
open its bowels). Buckets and scoops are provided at the shows,
but these are not always situated where you want them. If you have
your own bags it saves time, and you can then dispose of the
bag at the appropriate bins. You will be fined if you do not
clear up after your dog.

It may seem that you have a car-full when you are setting off to a show, but it is
better to be prepared. A lead is one of the most important items. Some exhibitors use
a special show lead, available in a variety of colours, so they can match the lead with
the outfit they are wearing. I prefer to use a plain leather lead and choke chain. I
think this looks smarter on a Weimaraner, but it is all a matter of personal taste. If

Ireland's first Champion: Ir. Ch. Arras Attack of Trilite. Irish breed record holder with with 23 major Green Stars and also field qualified.

you show your dog you must not leave a collar on it all the time as this will mark the dog's neck. The only time it needs to wear a collar is when it is benched. You must not forget your own appearance on the day of the show. There are no hard and fast rules regarding dress in the ring, but you should look neat and tidy, and you should not wear anything that will detract from your dog, such as clashing colours or a flowing skirt. You will probably have to travel some distance in the car to get to a show, so make sure you choose a fabric that does not crease, and one that is easy to wash. You can get quite dirty by the the end of the day, and you don't want to spend a fortune on dry-cleaning bills. A lot of women wear trousers, as these are more practical, but if you prefer to wear a skirt it should be of reasonable length as you will have to bend over your dog. Sensible shoes are a must, as you will be spending hours on your feet, either chatting to friends or watching the judging, before you even step foot in the ring. When you are in the ring you will have to run with your dog, so you need shoes that will stay on your feet! Men can look smart in a jacket or body-warmer and trousers, but if you wear a tie, make sure it is pinned down so it does not flap when you are running or bending over your dog. Showing can be an expensive business, particularly at Championship show level, so make sure you give yourself every chance of success. Professional handlers dominate the show scene in America; this is not the case in Britain, though they are more prevalent in some breeds than others. There are a number of Weimaraners that are professionally handled, and these dogs are usually presented to perfection. If you are competing seriously, you must make sure that your dog is shown with equal skill. The better you show your dog, the more chance you have of being placed. This does not mean that you have to bath your dog every time you go to a show, but it must be given a good brush to get rid of any dried mud or loose hairs. If you own a long-coat you will need to do some extra work. Trim around the feet and along the line of the hocks to give a neater appearance. If you are not confident about doing this, ask someone who shows a long-coat for advice. Comb out any dead hair, and if the coat looks dull, try adding a coat conditioner to the dog's food. However, be careful with all additives as they can upset the natural balance of the diet. It may be worth trying a different brand of dog food, as they do vary in their effect on a dog's coat. Some feeds can make a Weimaraner's coat harsh, some can make it soft, and others can even make it darker in colour. You must find out what suits your dog: if you want to get the best out of your Weimaraner, you have to put the best in.

Avoid using titbits when you are in the ring; baiting is frowned upon in Weimaraners. A judge will penalise a dog as having a bad temperament if it is constantly being fed, particularly when the judge is going over it. Handlers sometimes resort to baiting when a dog is inclined to growl or snap, but this tendency is totally unacceptable in a Weimaraner. If you take the time to train your dog properly at home and at ringcraft classes, it should behave well in the ring without the need for titbits. When your class has finished and the judging has been completed you can praise your dog and reward it with a titbit, if you like.

When you are in the ring, the procedure is more or less the same at all levels of shows. The steward will call your class and exhibitors will be asked to stand with their dogs in a row. The judge will walk up and down and look at all the dogs present. He or she will then call each exhibitor and will 'go over' each dog in turn. Keep an eye on what the judge is doing – don't allow yourself to be distracted, chatting to the other exhibitors – and be ready when the judge calls you. Then, walk briskly towards the judge and pose your dog, making sure it is standing with a straight front and looking its best. The judge will probably walk round the dog to inspect conformation, then most judges will start at the mouth and work their way down the dog's body, running their hands over its body, and finishing at the hindquarters. When the judge moves to the rear of the dog, you must move to the front; this should steady the dog and stop it fidgeting. Command your dog to stand

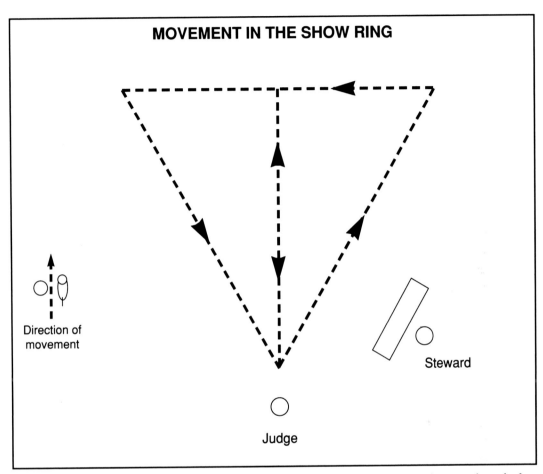

MOVEMENT IN THE SHOW RING

Direction of movement

Steward

Judge

still, you cannot expect the dog to behave unless it is told what to do – and no judge will penalise an exhibitor for talking to his or her dog!

After the judge has finished going over your dog, you will be asked to move it. If you are not clear about what the judge has said, ask again, so you set off with confidence. Gather up the lead and run out in the direction indicated by the judge. Most judges ask you to move in a triangle, and then straight up and down, as this gives them the opportunity view the dog from all angles. Move fluently, and when you come to the corners and the turns, try to negotiate them neatly, guiding your dog around them. The idea is to keep the dog on the move, and not to keep stopping and starting with each change of direction, as this interrupts the dog's natural movement. You should be moving at a speed that suits your dog, and you must match your pace to the dog's gait. This requires a lot of practice before you get it right, but it is a real joy to watch a Weimaraner moving in unison with its handler in the ring, and it is well worth all the homework. When this exercise has been completed you will be asked to stand in line, until all the dogs have been assessed. Again, keep an eye on the judge, as he will have a last look at all the dogs when he has finished looking at each individual, and this could be vital when the judge is making his final decision. Make sure your dog is standing straight, and looking bright and alert. Whatever the outcome, praise your dog, and congratulate or commiserate with the other exhibitors. If you have not been placed, there is always another show tomorrow, and what one judge did not like today, another may admire the next time you are in the ring.

If you are travelling with children, pack a small bag for them. My six-year-old always takes her doll and its clothes, my son used to take his cars. Travelling can be very boring for small children and the toys will help to pass the time. Remember, children rarely have any choice about the day's activities, and so you will have to be patient, especially at the end of a long day. You can also buy small lunch-boxes and pack food and drink for them – kids always want a drink or something to eat the moment the car is moving! If your children are very small, carry a potty, as toilets are never around at the right time. Again, be organised. If I was leaving early in the morning I would put my daughter straight in the car in her nightclothes, wrapping her in a blanket. She would soon go back to sleep, and when we stopped later in the morning I would get her dressed. You must keep children under control at all times at the shows, and remember that not all people and dogs like them.

There may seem an awful lot to do and remember when you are showing, but as you gain experience in this pastime, things will become easier. Showing can be very rewarding. Of course, you will have good days and bad, but you must always be aware of the needs of your dog, and above all, you should try to make it an enjoyable day out for all concerned.

Chapter Nine

JUDGING

Nobody can become a judge overnight, no matter how keen you are to get involved in this side of the show world. It is not sufficient to own and exhibit a Weimaraner: you must have a thorough all-round knowledge of the breed, you must be able to spot different types, and you must be able to assess a dog's faults and qualities against the Breed Standard. It is important to remember that everyone has their own opinions, and one judge may penalise a fault more harshly than another – that is the essence of competing in the show ring. If everyone shared the same viewpoint, there could only be one winner, and that would mean no more shows and no more judges.

As you spend more time at shows you will be able to watch judges at work, but don't focus on your own breed alone: have a look at how other breeds are judged in the ring. Every show requires stewards, and this is a useful opportunity to get inside the ring, without your dog. You can watch the dogs being judged at close quarters, and you can talk to the judge. Wait until judging is completed and then you can ask why certain dogs have been placed. Some judges will be more helpful than others, but if you find someone who is willing to talk, listen to what they have to say and weigh it up against your own opinion. This is a job where you need to know your

Sh. Ch. Hansom Misty Blue: This bitch appeared in a television advertising campaign. Owned and bred by Mr R. M. W. Finch.

own mind, so you are confident about picking the dogs you like. Judging seminars are very useful, and these are organised by breed clubs, societies and gundog clubs. The aim is not necessarily to agree with the speaker, but to provoke an informed discussion on the breed concerned. You can very often learn more from the questions that are asked than from what the speaker has to say. I subscribe to the commonly held belief that good judges are born, not made. However, you can always learn something new, and if you attend shows, seminars and any other function where dog people meet, you will improve your knowledge of dogs. You must also acquaint yourself with Kennel Club rules and regulations for judges – and keep reading the Breed Standard so you know it intimately.

The next step is to be invited to judge by a canine society. Again, do not try to rush into this by making yourself available before you are ready; wait until you feel

Sh. Ch. Sally's Secret J.W.: Winner of 6 CCs. Owned by Mr R. Clarke. Bred by Mrs Swain.

completely confident. When you accept a judging appointment you must agree to abide by the rules laid down by the society, and you will also agree to turn up on the day. If you fail to do this, without good reason, you will be reported to the Kennel Club. About a week before the show you will receive details of your entries, how many dogs are entered in each class (the dogs' names and owners will not be given), and what time you will be required to arrive. On the day of the show you must make sure you arrive in good time and report to the secretary. You will be told what ring you will be judging in, and who will be stewarding for you. You should dress smartly, and women should avoid wearing short skirts, as judges need to bend over the dogs they are assessing. Wear something comfortable and practical. Judging can be tiring, particularly on the feet, so wear sensible shoes. Handling a class of dogs can be quite a mucky business, especially if you get a few dribbly dogs – so take some hand-wipes with you. You will also need a pen, as you will need to write critiques of the first prize winners after every class. These are recorded in the judge's book, which lists all your classes and the dogs' numbers. It will also have a couple of judge's slips, which you have to tear out and sign for the award boards and for the show secretary. The judge's book does not contain the dogs' names, or the names of breeders and owners. At the end of the day, you are allowed to keep the judge's book, which should record the number of dogs in each class and absentees, and you will be given a marked up catalogue so you can complete your critiques for the dog

Sh. Ch. Gunalt Cacharel: Winner 16 CCs. Owned and bred by Mr and Mrs S. Hollings.

papers. Critiques should be kept brief, and always try to be constructive in your criticism. Do not make the sort of negative comments about dogs or owners that could cause bad feeling. From the day of your first judging appointment, keep a record of all your appointments, and the numbers of dogs you have judged. If you move up the judging scale and receive an invitation to judge at a Championship show, you will have to fill in a detailed questionnaire for the Kennel Club. Judging at a Championship show means that you will be awarding the coveted Challenge Certificates, and so the Kennel Club Judges Committee must give its formal approval. The completed questionnaire must be submitted to the Kennel Club well before the proposed judging appointment, and often the applicant is turned down in the first instance. This means the budding Championship show judge must go through the whole procedure again. The minimum qualifications are five years judging experience in the breed, and you must have judged at least 250 dogs. The committee may also write to the breed clubs that have invited you to judge for comments on your judging ability.

Whatever level of show you are judging, the essentials remain the same: you are in the ring to judge the good and bad points of a breed, and you must know whether a dog conforms to the Breed Standard. The people who show under you have paid for your opinion, so be pleasant and give every dog the same amount of time. Be careful not to appear too friendly, as this could give the wrong impression. Equally, never apologise for the decisions you have made – you must have confidence in the reasons why you made your placings. Obviously you cannot please everyone, but if you have done your homework, the best dogs on the day will have been placed.

When I am judging I like to see handlers showing well-presented, nicely-behaved dogs. If the dog stands well and is easy to go over, it makes the judge's job so much easier. If you spend time training your dog to stand still, and to run out at a pace which suits dog and handler, it could well result in a higher placing in the show ring. The dog that is constantly messing about is not doing itself any favours. Of course, you can excuse a puppy that fidgets, especially if you are judging a big class which can be quite time-consuming, but adult dogs should behave at all times in the ring. There is nothing worse than having a fully-grown Weimaraner leaping about when you are trying to inspect its mouth, and shyness in this breed cannot be tolerated. Remember that when you are judging you may be influencing the future of the breed, for the winners you select may well be producing the Weimaraners of the next generation. So therefore it is essential that you penalise dogs that carry bad faults or undesirable character traits that could be inherited. The dogs that you place should be the soundest and the best specimens that are available to you on the day. Judging can be highly educational – you can learn a lot from going over a dog, rather than just viewing it from afar. It can also be very rewarding, especially if you see your Best of Breed winner going on to become Best in Show.

Ch. Monroes Ambition of Westglade jumps clear. Owner: Gwen Sowersby. Breeder: John Matusezwska.

Chapter Ten

AGILITY AND OBEDIENCE

GENERAL CONTROL

Control is essential for all dogs. It is the foundation for a career in Field Trials, Working Trials, Obedience and Agility, and it is a prerequisite to the peace of mind of the pet owner. Weimaraners should be socialized with people and other dogs at an early age, and they should accept being handled. The handler should run his hands over his dog and inspect its mouth gently, on a daily basis. The dog should also learn its place in the family 'pack'. The Weimaraner can be a very dominant animal and will try to climb up in pecking order. It should, therefore, learn to be obedient to basic commands, irrespective of whether there is an intention to continue into the more advanced areas of work. When an adorable little Weimaraner puppy is brought to its new home, the owner should remember that it will grow into an adolescent with alarming speed! Rules need to be established, and a little foresight, together with the enforcement of the basic rules, will save many tears at a later date. Handlers

Beckstone Envoy CDex., UDex.,WDex., TDex competing in Obedience Trials at Crufts.   *Ann Cook*

can be tempted to resort to harsh handling when they try and correct ingrained bad habits.

Most Weimaraners are slow to mature, both mentally and physically, so it is important to keep early lessons simple and short. The handler should decide which simple task he wishes his dog to perform, he should be consistent in his use of commands, and he should always be in a position to gently enforce the command, if necessary. When the dog has performed the exercise it should be rewarded with the handler's praise. Initially only one exercise should be attempted at a time, in order to avoid confusion, and the training session should finish with a game before the dog gets bored. A dog should not be expected to work on a full stomach; at least one hour, preferably longer, should elapse between feeding and exercise. If your Weimaraner is to be trained for competitive work, it is essential that instant obedience is not achieved at the expense of its instinctive enthusiasm for its work. The greatest pleasure in owning a dog is when the handler and dog work as a closely-knit partnership. This bonding can be achieved only if the handler is prepared to put in as much effort as the dog. Play is essential in the development of the Weimaraner's character; the dog should enjoy playing games, but on the handler's terms. If these games involve toys, the handler should always finish the game in possession of the toy while the dog is still interested in it. Great care should be taken when playing retrieving games – many dogs have lost their lives through swallowing a ball or spearing their throat with the sharp end of a stick. If the games involve running about, it is the dog that should run after the handler, and not the other way round – this will help in the recall exercise. It is inadvisable for a novice handler to encourage a Weimaraner to use its teeth on their own person or their clothing, even in play.

Ideally, a Weimaraner should be happy to play socially with other dogs when it is being exercised, and it should be allowed to exploit its wonderful sense of smell. It should, however, prefer to be doing things with the handler. This will involve the handler in playing with the dog when out for exercise, rather than merely walking to the park and reading a newspaper until the dog decides it is time to go home! It is a good idea to enrol at a reputable training class where help is at hand to nip any problems in the bud. With the best will in the world, *all* handlers make mistakes and need help to sort out the ensuing problems.

COMPETITIVE OBEDIENCE

Competitive obedience is the canine equivalent of dressage for horses. Great emphasis is placed on precision and the handler must have an eye for detail. For example, the handler must not be content if his dog sits fairly quickly and roughly in the right place, as his dog will be penalised if it hesitates at all before it sits, or if it sits crooked. Most Weimaraners are at a slight disadvantage in obedience competitions as their sleek outline and lack of hair ensure that the slightest inaccuracies are noticed!

HEELWORK: This is probably the exercise to which most importance is attached. The dog will be required to maintain a consistent position with the handler throughout the test, including changes in direction, and it must sit immediately without losing its position when the handler halts. In the higher classes the heelwork will include changes of speed and the dog will be expected to work without extra commands from the handler. The dog will eventually have to give his handler 100 per cent attention for up to ten minutes of heelwork, which is not as easy as it sounds among all the distractions of a busy showground.

In order to appreciate the required standard, it is a good idea to go to an obedience show as a spectator, and you will be able to see the progression through the various classes. However, do not come away from the showground with the attitude that your dog will never be able to do that. There is no such word as 'can't' in dog training – unless there is a physical constraint. A handler who has already achieved a good working partnership with his dog – achieving control without losing willingness to play – is at a tremendous advantage when training the heelwork exercise. The dog will already be willing to give its attention to its handler, and the handler can use play to relieve any tension caused by the need to insist on precision.

RETRIEVE: The dog will be required to retrieve various articles without damaging them. The most reliable retrieving dogs are those which have been taught to hold articles properly, rather than those that chase a moving article with the intention of 'killing' it or playing with it. The handler who has accustomed his dog to gentle handling of the mouth should have little trouble in persuading his dog to hold various articles without chewing them or spitting them out. This exercise should not be introduced until the dog has finished teething, so that there is no danger of tender gums. Difficult articles, such as metal, should not be introduced until the dog is happily retrieving easier articles. Dangerous articles, i.e. those which could be swallowed or those which could splinter, should be avoided.

SCENT DISCRIMINATION: Scent discrimination is where the dog is required to identify and retrieve a cloth bearing the scent of its handler (or the judge in the highest class) out of up to nine other cloths. This exercise should pose few problems for the Weimaraner that has been taught the retrieve exercise properly, as it has an excellent sense of smell. Handlers who wish their Weimaraners to compete in Working Trials as well as in obedience should take care that they set their dogs up for the scent exercise in a different way to their property search set-up. They should also ensure that one exercise is understood thoroughly before introducing the other.

STAYS: It is important to have a dog which is reliable in the stay exercises. The 'stay' should have formed part of the basic control training of the dog from an early age. It is interesting to note that many of the dogs which are unreliable in the stay exercises (particularly where the handler must go out of sight) are those which sleep in the handler's bedroom and are rarely left on their own!

TRAINING CLUBS: Handlers who wish to train their dogs for competitive Obedience are strongly advised to join a good training club where the members have a good success rate in *all* the classes at open/championship obedience show level. Expert tuition and examples to follow will therefore be available. Be prepared,

Weimaraners are naturally agile and athletic. *Ann Cook.*

however, to select the methods most suitable to you and your dog from a wealth of often conflicting methods. A list of registered training clubs can be obtained from the Kennel Club. Alternatively many vets or the police will be able to give you the necessary information. It is a good idea to go and watch a few classes before joining, as some clubs are better than others.

AGILITY TESTS

The Kennel Club describes Agility Tests as 'fun competitions', and they were introduced as a demonstration event at Crufts in 1978. Agility has since mushroomed as a competitive sport, and thirty entries per class is not uncommon. Indeed, some classes, such as the qualifying classes for the Olympia Christmas Horse Show in London, may attract entries of over 500 dogs! There is no doubt that most of the dogs competing in Agility Tests consider it to be great fun, and the Weimaraner is no exception – it is a natural athlete provided it is not asked to jump on a full stomach.

AGE: It is inadvisable for any dog to start any training which involves jumping before its bones have had a chance to harden properly. No dog should start training over obstacles before it is twelve months old, and it is advisable with large dogs, such as Weimaraners, to wait a few months after their first birthday. All dogs must be at least eighteen months old before they can compete in Agility Tests or Working Trials, due to the potential damage that jumping can cause to a young dog's bone structure.

CONTROL: It is essential to have a reasonable standard of control over the dog before introducing it to agility training. Once the dog has gained its confidence over the agility equipment, it will be tempted to invent its own courses which will lead to elimination and much handler-frustration!

HURDLES: (2ft 6ins maximum height) and tyres (3ft to centre). Hurdles should present few problems to the Weimaraner as it is a naturally agile breed. Hurdles and the tyre should be introduced at a low height and gradually increased to the maximum height. Once the dog is jumping with confidence, the handler should introduce jumps of different types (providing they are safe), and this should ensure that the dog will jump over single bar hurdles, rather than running underneath them. The dog should be taught to take hurdles from different angles as this can save vital seconds in a competition – handlers are advised to watch the top show jumpers in action for tips on cutting corners. The dog should be given as much experience as possible through different tyres as it will encounter many different tyres throughout its career. A dog should never be asked to jump a tyre at an angle, which could risk injury to the dog.

CONTACT POINT EQUIPMENT: The dog must make 'contact' with the beginning and end of the 'A' frame, the dog-walk and the see-saw. To teach a long-striding dog, such as the Weimaraner to do this will take patience and control. The dog that will stop when it is told, will be easier to teach to make the contacts. Some Weimaraners, especially if they are fairly broad specimens, may take some time to gain confidence on the dog-walk and see-saw. These pieces of equipment may only be nine inches wide, so the dog will have to learn to walk on a narrow gauge in a similar way to a tight-rope performer. Contact point equipment should rarely be approached at an angle, as this can result in injury to the dog.

TUNNELS: Once an initial reluctance to go through the tunnels is overcome, the problem will be to prevent the dog diving through the tunnel at every opportunity! The flat tunnel (where the dog must learn to run into the dark) should be introduced after the dog is happily running through the pipe tunnel. A sociable dog can often be

Negotiating the see-saw.   *Ann Cook.*

taught to follow another dog through a tunnel, without realising what it has done. Alternatively, the dog is held at one end of a short pipe tunnel while the handler crouches at the other end and calls the dog. It is important that the dog can only see the handler's face if it looks through the tunnel, so it may have to be put into the 'down' position with the handler in a similar position at the other end (preferably on dry ground!). Be careful not to use the same command for tunnels as for the tyre (e.g. 'through').

WEAVING POLES: In order to win in Agility, the dog must be very fast in the weaving poles. It must be taught to enter the weaves correctly on its own, from any angle. This takes a great deal of practice and it is essential that you practise at home, in between the usual club training sessions. Assuming the dog is on the left of the handler, it must enter the poles away from the handler between the first and second pole.

SAFETY: There is a slight risk that a dog might get injured when doing Agility; this risk will be minimised by careful training and by careful handling. The handler should ensure that he does not put his dog over unsound equipment and should inspect the equipment before running his dog in training or at a show.

TRAINING CLUBS: Most people who wish to train their dogs to do Agility will have to join a club, due to the specialised equipment involved. Many clubs provide both Obedience and Agility training.

Working Trials Champion Ritisons Constellation: The first Weimaraner to be awarded this title in Britain. Owned by Jenny Wilson.

Chapter Eleven

WORKING TRIALS

By Jean Fawkes

The Weimaraner is ideally suited to field work because of its strong build, its keen sense of smell, and its willingness to please. A well-trained Weimaraner will always give its best, and can compete successfully against all other breeds. Weimaraners are quick to learn – but never try to rush the training. This should be a gradual process, and every stage should be perfected before moving on to the next. If you try to take short-cuts in gundog training, you will only find that you have to return to the basics. The first, and most important consideration is the dog that you are planning to train. There is no point in spending eighteen months training a dog that has hip trouble or any other problem which might affect its working ability. If you are buying a puppy for work, make sure you go to a breeder where the parents have been hip-scored. Ideally, the puppy should come from lines that have dogs with proven working ability in their pedigrees – for example, Field Trial winners or dogs

Working Trials involve three disciplines:

CONTROL: Recall: Jenny Belmont with Beckstone Hilda's Megan. CDex., UDex., WDex.

Retrieving a dumb-bell.

TRACKING: Weimaraners make excellent tracking dogs.

AGILITY: The long-jump.

which have obtained Working Trial qualifications. When you have selected the right dog you should find a training class which specialises in Field Trials or Working Trials. These can vary in standard, and so it is a good idea to find about the tutor's qualifications before you join. The advantage of attending classes is that extensive space and specialised equipment is required, and the experienced teacher will help you to correct any bad habits from an early stage. The training club will advise you of the best age to start training your dog. Safety is a very important consideration – both for you and your dog – and equipment should be checked at each session it is used.

Working Trials for dogs are the equivalent to three-day eventing for horses. They are both minority sports that are officially licensed and run under strict rules. For the dogs, the tests of control and obedience – comparable to dressage – and the agility, which is comparable to show jumping, are performed under one judge. The canine equivalent of the cross-country section of eventing is a half-mile track in open country, and a search for articles within a marked area. In order to succeed in either sport, the animal must be of suitable physique, ability and temperament – and the same can be said of the rider or handler! The dog will be expected to be lead-free most of the time, and so basic obedience is vital. If your dog it not obedient on the lead, there is little chance of it obeying comands when it is free. It will probably take

Father and son: Miroku Argos CDex., UDex.,TDex., (left) and Salvomist Choice UDex.,WDex. and winner of the 1985 Bruno Trophy. Owned by Ted Rowley.

you eighteen months to two years to train your dog to a reasonable standard to compete in Working Trials, so you need time and patience. It is important to develop good co-ordination between dog and handler, and Weimaraners have a tendency to keep their distance from you when they doing heel-work, unlike a Border Collie which will keep in very close. This tendency has to be corrected, and practice is usually the only solution to the problem. The Weimaraner is strong in physique and substance, and so it will make light work of scales and jumps. However, it cannot be stressed enough that a dog must not be jumped before its bones are set – usually after its first birthday. Some Weimaraners are slow to mature, so always err on the side of caution.

One of the attractions of Working Trials is that it is competitive, with prizes awarded to the first three in each stake; but a certificate is also presented to every dog that obtains the requisite percentage of total marks allotted to the stake, regardless of the number of entries. Working Trials are licensed by the Kennel Club as Open or Championship events. The Certificate of Merit that is awarded in each stake at Open level (except in the Companion Dog stake) is the 'pass' required for entry into the same stake at a Championship Trial, and into the higher grade at an Open Trial. The Qualifying Certificate that is awarded in each stake at a

Krijac's Blazing Thor: CDex., UDex., WDex., TDex.

Owned by Chris Sullivan and Miss J. Mason.

Ch. Reeman Aruac: CDex., UDex., WDex., TDex. Owned and trained by Bob Lynch.

Championship Trial states that the dog has successfully qualified in that grade, adding 'Excellent' when it has 80 per cent or above total marks. The top qualifications of 'Patrol Dog' (PD) – formerly 'Police Dog' – and 'Tracking Dog' (TD) are officially added to the registered name of the dog in the Kennel Club records and registers, and qualify the dog for entry in the Kennel Club Stud Book. It is customary for the owners of dogs that have qualified in any stake at a Championship Working Trial to add the grade of qualification when quoting the dog's name on a pedigree or entry form. This unofficial practice has not been censored.

Qualification has never been easy, and graduation through the different stakes is recognised as proof of real ability. There are five separate stakes, and the exercises in each stake are listed in groups. In order to qualify, 70 per cent of the marks in each group must be obtained, and then a total of 80 per cent of the marks allotted to that particular stake must be awarded.

The Companion Dog (CD) stake comprises four groups:

Control: heelwork on and off the lead, recall to handler and send away.
Stays: 'sit' 2 minutes and 'down' 10 minutes – the handler out of sight of the dog.
Agility: clear or hurdle jump, long jump and scale jump.
Retrieving and nosework: retrieve a dumb-bell and search for three articles within a marked area.

Small dogs are able to take part and qualify in this stake as the height of the jumps is varied according to the dog's shoulder height. The qualification 'CDex.' is not a compulsory requirement, neither does a dog obtain a Certificate of Merit in this stake at an Open Trial before being entered in a CD stake at a Championship Trial. Newcomers to trials are encouraged to gain experience by starting off in the CD stake at Open as well as Championship level.

The Utility Dog (UD) stake consists of three groups:

Control: Heel free, send away, retrieve a dumb-bell, down 10 minutes, and steady to gunshot.
Agility: 3ft clear jump, 9ft long jump, and 6ft scale jump. The dog is required to scale the obstacle on command and remain stationary on the far side until it is recalled over the scale by the handler.
Nosework: search for four articles placed within a 25-yard square, and a half-mile

Ch. Reeman Aruac CDex., UDex., WDex., TDex. Owned and trained by Bob Lynch.
track, half-an-hour old, with the track-layer's article at the end. The direction of the first leg of the track is indicated by a second marker placed some 30 yards from the starting pole.

A Certificate of Merit must be obtained in this stake at an Open Trial before a dog may enter the UD stake at a Championship Trial. When a dog has obtained a Certificate of Merit from the UD stake a dog may be entered in the **Working Dog (WD)** stake at an Open Trial. Here again, there are three groups:

Control: the same exercises as the UD stake.
Agility: the same exercises as the UD stake.
Nosework: As in the UD stake, there is a search for four articles placed within a 25-yard square, but the half-mile track is an hour-and-a-half-old and it has two articles laid on it, one of them at the end of the track. A single pole indicates the start of the track, and the dog must work out the direction from there of the first leg. One track article must be found for the dog to qualify, with, as usual, 70 per cent marks in each group and 80 per cent marks overall.

When a dog has been awarded the Certificate of Merit in a WD stake, and the qualification UDex. from a Championship Trial, it may enter the WD stake at a

Championship Trial. If the dog is successful and adds WDex. to its qualifications, it is eligible to compete in either of the top stakes. However, these became overcrowded in the early eighties, with many of the competitors clearly not ready for this level of competition. The result was that a doubling of the preliminary 'passes' at Open or Championship events has to be obtained before entry into either of these prestigious stakes. The highest level at which a dog may compete in Working Trials is for the qualification of Patrol Dog (PD) or Tracking Dog (TD) at a Championship event. The winner of either stake, providing it has the qualifying marks, is awarded the Kennel Club's Working Trial Certificate. If a dog achieves two such wins, under two different judges, it becomes Working Trial Champion (WTCh.).

The Tracking Dog (TD) stake has three groups:

Control: heel free, send away, and directional control, speak on command, down 10 minutes and steadiness to gunshot.
Agility: clear, long and scale jumps, as before.
Nosework: search for articles as previously, but on a half-mile track three hours old, with three articles laid on it. Again, a single pole indicates the start of the track. To qualify, two articles from the track must be found, plus the usual percentage of group and total marks.

The Patrol Dog (PD) stake consists of four groups:

Control: the same as for TD.
Agility: the same as for TD.
Nosework: the search for articles is also the same as TD (four articles in a 25-yard marked area, of which at least two must be found and brought out by the dog), but the half-mile track is two hours old, laid from a single pole and with two articles on it, one of which must be found in order to qualify.
Manwork: quartering the ground to locate a hidden person, a test of courage, search and escort of a 'criminal', recall from a running criminal, and the pursuit and detention of a criminal.

Manwork is part of the regular work of a police dog, but such specialised training requires great care and considerable skill by a civilian handler with a dog that is primarily a family pet. At the time of writing, the publicity concerning incidents where dogs have attacked and bitten children or innocent members of the public is arousing considerable 'anti-dog' prejudice. Every owner contemplating training his

Beckstone Hilda's Megan CDex., UDex., WDex.: Scotland's Weimaraner of the Year 1990, and Reserve Weimaraner of the Year 1990 in the Weimaraner Club of Great Britain awards.

Inmoor Solid Silver CDex., UDex., WDex., TDex., and winner of 2 RCC's in the show ring. Owned and bred by Mr and Mrs J. Carter.

dog for a PD qualification should be fully aware of his responsibility. However, a PD dog that is properly trained and in the right hands, is not vicious or trigger-happy when off duty. In order to enter the Tracking Dog stake at a Championship Trial (firstly to obtain the TDex. qualification, and then aiming for the WT Certificate), a dog must have qualified WDex. twice, achieving a Certificate of Merit on two occasions in the TD stake at an Open Trial. The same degree of competence is required for the PD stake at a Championship event, namely the two WDex. qualifying certificates, and two Certificates of Merit from the PD stake at an Open Trial. At present, there are roughly two TD Championship Trials for every PD Championship. Organising an Open or Championship event requires skilful management, a team of experienced and dedicated helpers, and plenty of ground. A trial is always run over a minimum of two days; a Tracking Dog Championship may attract so many entries that five or even six days are required for the nosework alone, as each dog needs half an hour to complete track and search, with a final day set aside for Control and Agility. Farmers are generally tolerant, and allow access to arable or grazing land when the fields are well started in growth or have been cut, or when their sheep and cattle can be moved elsewhere for a few days. National Trust, common land or heathland, if available, may bring possible hazards of ramblers and sheep, but the owners of private moorland are understandably reluctant to risk the disturbance to game. Thus Working Trials cannot proliferate like obedience or breed shows. Considerable physical effort and dedication is needed to train and prepare a dog for entry into a Working Trial, but all this is forgotten when a well-loved pet gains a certificate in any of the stakes. Disappointments are many, and failure can be due as much to the weather and ground conditions as to inadequate training, but the camaraderie that exists between trialists (who admit they must be a little mad to be in the sport at all) is notable. Good sportsmanship prevails, however bitter a disappointment on the day, and success, when it comes, is very sweet indeed.

Chapter Twelve

FIELD TRIALS

Field Trials differ from Working Trials as they use live game, and the tests take place in the field. This means that each test the dog is set is slightly different, as the game is unpredictable. The tests represent, as closely as possible, a day in the shooting field. As with all disciplines, control is essential and so basic obedience is the first step. The dog is expected to work off the lead most of the time, and this can only be achieved when a dog has been trained to be obedient on the lead and walking to heel. The dog must be steady to shot, and it should be able to retrieve from land or water. However, as soon as you are confident that your dog can retrieve, it is better to leave this out of training sessions until it has mastered the basics. There is no point having a dog that picks up a dummy, and then runs off and fails to return to the handler.

The Weimaraner is a Hunt, Point and Retrieve dog (H.P.R.) – the other groups are Retrievers, Spaniels, and Pointers and Setters. Each group has slightly different tasks that the dogs are expected to perform. H.P.R. dogs are required to hunt or quarter the ground until the game is found. Then they must point, and at command they must flush out the game. The game is then shot, and the dog must retrieve it. Field

Mr Harvey CDex., UDex., WDex. on the trail. Owned by Gwen Sowersby.

Trials consist of one or more Stakes, which constitute separate competitions at that Trial. The Stakes can be classified for Puppies, Novice, All-Aged or Open. In the Open Stakes dogs have the opportunity of gaining a qualification towards the title of Field Trial Champion, or towards entry in the Championships or Champion Stake for its breed. A dog receives an award if it is placed first, second, third or fourth in a Stake. A Diploma of Merit can be awarded at a Championship or Champion Stake meeting, and Certificates of Merit can be awarded in any other Stake. Dogs are run singly in order of their draw, under two judges, judging as a pair. A dog must have been tried at least twice in the line, excluding the water retrieve, before it may receive an award. In H.P.R. breeds eliminating faults are: hard mouth, whining or barking, flushing up-wind, out of control, running in or chasing, failure to hunt or point, missing game birds on the beat, refusal to retrieve or swim. Major faults are: not making good ground, missing game on the beat, unsteadiness, sticking on point, persistent false pointing, not acknowledging game going away, failing to find dead or wounded birds, catching unwounded game, disturbing ground, noisy handling, and changing game while retrieving.

Training should take place at specialised classes, but you will also need to put in a lot of practice at home in order to compete successfully. A dog will be required to be sent away to retrieve, and it must stop on command and be redirected to the left or

Father and Son: Miroku Argos CDex., UDex., TDex. (right) and Salvomist Choice working in the snow. Owned by Ted Rowley.

right. When the dog has picked up the dummy or game, it must be returned straight to the handler. This also requires a water retrieve, where the dog is expected to go in and through water, retrieve, and return straight to the handler. A dog must never get involved when other dogs are working, and it must be under control at all times. Retrieve training is best attempted in a controlled space such as a lane, or you could cut a path in a long patch of grass, and then place the dummy at one end. This encourages the dog to go straight to the dummy, and then return straight to you. When you graduate to teaching the dog to search for the dummy, it is best to use the corner of a field, or somewhere where the dog cannot run off in all directions. As with all training, you cannot run before you walk, and if you encounter problems with a particular task, then return to basics and start again. A Weimaraner is quick to learn what you require, but it can be equally quick to learn bad habits. There is therefore a danger in trying to move too fast. If, for example, a dog picks up a dummy and then runs off with it because it has not been taught to retrieve, it could take you weeks to correct the habit. So the golden rule is to take one step at a time, and get each step correct before moving on to the next.

Everybody has to start somewhere, and Janet Drury gives an illuminating account of her first experience in Field Trials with her long-haired Weimaraner called Duke.

" 'You ought to try working that dog – he's got a good nose,' an old hand remarked, as my dog Duke was merrily sniffing at the water rats down the river bank. I looked down at my pet, into his wonderfully alert face, and I realised I had never paid any attention to this particular feature. To be honest, my two year old Weimaraner was becoming quite headstrong, and I thought that some extra training would benefit us both. Fired up with enthusiasm I found a gundog training class and turned up one Sunday morning, a grey hairy dog and handler, without a whistle, rope lead, or Barbour – quite a spectacle amongst a line-up of sportsmen in green wellies with black Labradors!

"Duke had always been a keen retriever, fetching articles of laundry and other household items to embarrass and amuse us, especially in front of company. At the training class he proved quite a star, graduating from one class to the next, until one day, when Nigel, our teacher, decided to make life more interesting by using dead pigeons for the retrieves. Duke, true to form, sped off with great enthusiasm, reached the bird, had a good sniff, and cocked his leg over it –leaving a poor Labrador to fetch it! That was just the first of many such humiliations before an audience. My rising star then refused to retrieve outside, but he continued to shower us with items as soon as he was home again. My frustration with him did not help, but eventually I learnt one of my biggest lessons. When an aspect of training starts to go from bad to worse, stop there, and go back to the basics. If you try to force the issue, you will end up with a frayed temper and an unwilling dog. In fact, I have lost count of the times we have had to go back to square one. To overcome the problem with retrieves, we stopped all retrieving during training, and then after a while we reintroduced canvas dummies. We then graduated to fur and feather-covered dummies, then finally, I slipped in a dead pigeon and the problem was solved.

"When we reached the end of our training course, my teacher suggested that we should try to find a class for hunt, point and retrieve breeds, as opposed to Labrador Retriever types, as we now needed more ground in order to let Duke run free and strengthen his hunting ability. When I enquired about such classes and explained we had already been to a Labrador trainer, the experts shrieked in horror, insisting that I must have turned him into a retriever. To prove a point, we entered a Weimaraner Association assessment day. Duke, at the ripe old age of three, came out on top, and I realised that I was now on the brink of a whole new world. I was a complete novice; I didn't even know about caged game – but Duke did. He found and pointed all of the time. He was a natural good worker, full of potential, according to the assessor, Barbara Hargreaves – impaired only by his handler, she should have added!

"After that, there was no turning back. We went to training classes with the Weimaraner Association and Lindum Gundog Society, and we were encouraged to

Janet Drury with Duke.

Major on point.

enter a few working tests. My confidence grew with every prize we won, and by the time Duke was four we decided to think big and entered our first field trial. Well, what an eye-opener! I recommend anyone to try at least one field trial to experience that awful nerve-racking feeling! I switched into auto-pilot and Duke went out into the sugar beet like a trooper, methodically worked the woods and had a beautiful point on a pheasant, flushed to command, sat steady – and then disaster! The bird was shot out in the field, in full view of all the other competitors. In a daze I brought him back to heel and sent him for the retrieve. When he reached the pheasant he took one look at his audience and refused point-blank to pick it up. I was devastated – my wonderful dog, so keen at retrieving – what had caused him to turn off? The lesson to learn is that dogs are individuals and not machines, and sometimes things happen that you will never be able to explain.

"On another memorable occasion Duke had found a 'runner' and he remained staunch on point in a game strip, while another bird was put up, shot and landed in front of him. For the grand finale he did a spectacular 'run in' at the water retrieve before the gun had managed a shot, virtually retrieving the pigeon from mid-air! However, good times often followed bad, and I will always remember the shoot when Duke went on point in the middle of a very young field of rape. Assuming it must be a rabbit due to the lack of cover, I walked forward and ordered the flush. Up went a cock pheasant, which was shot way across the field. He marked it, and went straight into point again, in the same spot. Once again I ordered him to flush, imagining it to be a residual scent, but he produced two hen pheasants, and both were quite close this time. I turned to the guns to pick the cock pheasant, and they were only too pleased to oblige; so, praying that Duke had remembered the point of fall, I sent him out. What a gamble, but what a spectacular retrieve! Everyone was quite amazed, and I filled with pride when a 'gun' said we had made his season.

"So if your dog has the ability to work, let him, and if you have nerves of steel, trial him. If you are serious, it means joining virtually every Hunt, Point, Retrieve Club in order to keep in touch with dates and venues. You also need to enter every possible trial, as only twelve dogs complete the draw. You need to be a good map-reader, and you must be willing to travel from John o'Groats to Land's End at a moment's notice. It also helps if you are able to suppress all human emotions such as anger, frustration, disappointment, pride and excitement, as I am not sure which is worse, to be eliminated after two minutes, or reach the end of the trial without an award. However, you must always remember that this is a sport, which you, and your dog, should enjoy. There are two important lessons to learn: never take your eyes off your dog, and try to read body language. My first Weimaraner is still teaching me so much about the working strain – I often wonder if I will ever

Duke and Major: Both dogs enjoy nothing better than a day in the field.

completely understand him. Each time out is a new experience, and I never dreamt that a tubby bundle of trouble would change my life, and open so many doors. Looking at him now, stretched out in front of the fire, I wonder if he realises how much richer life has been because of him. And now the legend continues with his son, a constant companion and trialist – Major!"

Ch. Greywind's Jack Frost SD, CD, BROM: National Specialty winner and Best in Show.
                                                                    Bruce Harkins

Chapter Thirteen

THE WEIMARANER IN AMERICA

By Carole L. Richards

What is it like to own and compete with a Weimaraner in the U.S.A.? In fact, many people in the United States do not know what a Weimaraner is. If you are walking down an American street with your Weimaraner you will frequently be stopped and questioned as to what breed it is. One thing is certain, you will rarely get a neutral reaction to your grey friend. The breed is not one of the most popular in the States, ranking about fortieth in terms of numbers among the one hundred and thirty-one breeds currently recognised by the American Kennel Club. In a typical month some two-hundred and seventy Weimaraners are registered with the American Kennel Club, from total monthly registrations of more than 100,000 for all breeds. One of

Ch. Colsidex Standing Ovation BROM (left) is the top winning show Weimaraner of all time in America. He has also been the most influential sire. His offspring have dominated the show scene in the eighties and the Top Ten listing of Weimaraners has become a listing of his progeny. He is pictured with one of his daughters – Ch. Walhallas Zara vd Hoch Essen NSD,CD, V.BROM. They give a very clear picture of the male and female versions of the American show Weimaraner today.

the greatest attributes of the Weimaraner is its versatility, and for those who want to take part in competitions there is rarely a weekend where you are not able to participate in a dog show, field trial, hunting test, or some other formal event. In 1989 there were a total of 2,634 A.K.C. dog shows, 1,723 obedience trials, 215 tracking tests, 1,192 field trials and 6,204 hunting tests. This does not include the less formal activities such as seminars, or the many obedience tests, show handling classes, search and rescue work, hunting, tracking, and matches – where no championship points are on offer because they are practice shows. In *The Gazette*, the American Kennel Club's monthly magazine, it was stated that there were a total of 1,608,858 dogs competing in A.K.C. events in 1989.

The most popular activity is showing dogs at bench shows, and in an average year some 18,000 new Champions will be made up from all recognised breeds. It is reckoned to be a good year if about 180 of these are new Weimaraner Champions. Shows are organised by All Breed Clubs, which are dog clubs that may have

Ch. Valmar's Pollyanna BROM National Specialty winner, and typical of the type of Weimaraner bred in the western United States. *Bruce Harkins.*

fanciers of many, or all, of the breeds recognised by the American Kennel Club among their members, and by Specialty Clubs, where membership is restricted to devotees of a single breed. A large All Breed Club will usually hold two shows a year; a Speciality Club will restrict itself to one show. Specialty Clubs may hold their show in conjunction with an All Breed Club, or they may do it independently. Most shows are held on Saturdays or Sundays, and for convenience they are often held by two clubs at the same site – one on Saturday and one on Sunday. This increases the number of entries and cuts down on travel time. There are also show circuits where there may be six or seven shows in a row. These shows may be in different locations but within relatively close proximity, such as the Florida circuit, held each January. Some circuits have the same site which is shared by a different host club each day, like the Kentucky or Texas circuits. Many clubs hire a professional Superintendent to handle the business aspects of organising and conducting the show. A Superintendent (there are about a dozen for the U.S.A.) will send out advance publicity for the show, called a premium list, accept the entries, prepare award ribbons and rosettes, publish a catalogue of the entered dogs, maintain records of the day's activities, and contract for tenting and other ring equipment. Club members are usually responsible for trophies and catalogue advertising, supplying luncheon and/or dinner for the judges, making an application to the A.K.C. for the event and reporting on the event to the A.K.C., providing stewards to assist the judges in the ring, contracting with dog supply vendors for space to show their wares to spectators, directing the parking of cars, and collecting admission fees from spectators.

If you plan to exhibit your Weimaraner, the first step is to get information about shows and make an entry. Publicity on shows may be found from many sources. Superintendents will provide you with information on the shows for which they are hired, the American Kennel Club publishes a monthly listing of events (including shows, obedience trials and field activities), and various dog magazines and newsletters also have information on forthcoming shows. After you have participated in a few shows your name is included in the regular mailing lists that are maintained by the various Superintendents. The Superintendents will send a five or six page premium list, which lists the date, location and judges for a particular show. It gives information on trophies that are on offer and is accompanied by several entry forms. Generally, entries must be received by the host club (or the Superintendent if one has been hired for the function) at least two and a half weeks prior to the show. The closing date for entries is published in the premium list and on the entry form. The entry form, one page in length, requires the breed, name of dog, its parentage, registration number, class in which it is entered, date of birth, breeder, owner, handler, and where the confirmation of entry should be sent. This form must be sent with the entry fee to the address given on the entry form. Entry fees in the late eighties and early nineties were close to $20. For some shows such as the Westminster Dog Show it was $35. Some Superintendents offer a phone-in system where you can call a toll-free number and make your entries. In order to use this service there is an annual fee and you must register information on each dog with the Superintendent, prior to making entries. There is also a fee added to the basic entry fee for each show in which the dog is entered. Approximately a week before the date of the show you will receive your confirmation of entry. The confirmation identifies the dog, gives the armband number and includes a judging schedule. This gives the times each breed will be judged, any changes from the originally advertised judging panel, directions to the show, nearby hotels which accept dogs, and general information on the conduct of a show.

At most shows judging starts between 8.30 and 9.00 am. Shows may be held indoors or outside, depending on the time of year and the choice of the host club. Generally, when the season of the year permits, clubs will opt for an outside site.

Ch. Walhallas Zara vd Hoch Essen NSD, CD, NRD, V, BROM: Futurity winner. This bitch, owned by Carole Richards, typifies the type of Weimaraner that wins puppy competitions. John L. Ashby

These are often located at fairgrounds, on college campuses or in parks. Indoor locations include professional sporting event arenas, school gymnasiums, and hotel conference halls. At the outdoor shows, large brightly coloured tenting is usually provided over a portion of the ring, and there is a large central tent that is several hundred feet long. The centre of the long tent is kept as an open aisle, with rings radiating out on either side. Rings are divided by low folding wooden fencing and the judge and steward have a small table and chairs for their use in the ring. In addition, there are smaller tents for the host club officials, judges, the Superintendents, A.K.C. officials, and trophy committee. Many shows rent space to vendors who set up displays of their wares. All kind of things are offered for sale: collars, leads, dog food, dog toys, grooming supplies, clothing with pictures of your favourite breed, gold jewellery depicting all breeds, prints, porcelain dog figures, antiques and more dog paraphernalia than can be imagined. Food trucks arrive and offer breakfast and lunch. Hot-dogs and hamburgers are the mainstay, but other sandwiches, doughnuts, candy bars, ice-cream, coffee and sodas are also on sale to the hungry exhibitor. The car parking is another sight to behold. Dog show vehicles come in every shape and size. There are large mobile homes and recreational vehicles that people will live in while they are on the road, and some of the professional handlers have full-sized buses that have been converted into living space and kennel space. Some of the larger vehicles are luxurious with complete living quarters including kitchens with fridges, stoves, and microwave ovens, full bathroom facilities, comfortable bedrooms, air-conditioning and television. Vans and mini-vans are common, and these are usually crammed with dog crates, tack boxes, dog equipment, changes of clothes and stacks of old dog magazines, premium lists and flyers about yet another show. People with smaller breeds or only one or two dogs may also come in their passenger cars. Many exhibitors put signs on their vehicles with their kennel or breed name.

Show catalogues are on sale on the day, and these will inform exhibitors who they will be competing against. A judge may be assigned up to 175 dogs to judge in a day. Most assignments are less than that, but on the average a judge can expect to be working for several hours. The stewards arrive at the ringside shortly before the first class is scheduled to enter and arrange the ribbons and exhibitor armbands on the table that has been provided in their ring. Likewise, the judge will arrive prior to judging and inspect the ring to make sure its condition and configuration is acceptable, noting the presence of any holes, length of grass, or slope of the ground. The judge will decide on the best gaiting pattern to use in the ring, depending on all these factors. Exhibitors are expected to arrive early enough to check in with the steward and get their armband numbers. The armband numbers correspond to the numbers assigned to the dogs and published in the show catalogue. Shows are officially begun with the playing of the national anthem, usually a recording that is played over a loud-speaker system. All movement stops as the music begins and people and dogs stand to attention. At the conclusion of the music, the bustle resumes. The dog classes are judged first, then the bitches, and finally the Champions enter the ring. One Weimaraner is picked as the Best of Breed and will be eligible to compete in the Group. When judging of the breed is over, and if the judge's schedule permits, the professional photographer is called to the ring and the winners for the day may have a photo taken with their dog and the judge. The Weimaraner that has been undefeated by any other of his or her breed, i.e. the Weimaraner picked as Best of Breed, is eligible to compete for the Sporting Group. There are twenty-four breeds eligible: Brittanys, Pointers, German Shorthaired Pointer, German Wirehaired Pointer, Chesapeake Bay Retrievers, Curly Coated, Flatcoat and Golden Retriever, Labrador, English Setters, Irish and Gordon Setters, American Water Spaniel, Clumber Spaniels, Cocker Spaniels, English Springer Spaniels, Field Spaniels, Irish Water Spaniels, Sussex Spaniels, Welsh Springer Spaniels, Vizslas, Weimaraners and Wirehaired Pointing Griffons. The group judging is late in the day, usually when most if not all the breed judging has been completed. There are seven Groups: Sporting, Hound, Working, Terrier, Toy, Non-Sporting, and Herding. Usually they are judged one at a time so that spectators can watch each Group. There are four placements made in each group, and the winner of each group goes on to the judging for Best in Show.

TITLES USED IN THE U.S.A.

The titles preceding and following the names of American Weimaraners are either those awarded by the American Kennel Club or those awarded by the Weimaraner Club of America. They are divided into three categories: Bench, Field, and Obedience.

AMERICAN KENNEL CLUB TITLES

BENCH

CHAMPION (CH)

The title of Champion is attained by competing against other Weimaraners in the show ring. The first stage of the competition is against dogs of the same sex who have not yet attained the title of Champion and have been judged to be the best non-Champion dog or bitch entered at the show. Dogs compete separately from bitches, and a Winners Dog and Winners Bitch are selected at each show. Both Winners Dog and Winners Bitch then have the opportunity to compete against any Champions entered at the show. The selection is then made for: Best of Breed, Best Opposite Sex (to the dog/bitch selected as Best of Breed) and Best of Breed Winners (either the Winners Dog or Winners Bitch). Championship points are awarded on the basis of the number of dogs competing. There are eleven geographic divisions for the U.S.A. and one for Puerto Rico. The number of points varies according to the number competing, and the geographic location of the show. There must be competition within the same sex for the Winners Dog or Winners Bitch to be awarded a point. A maximum of five points may be won at a show. A total of fifteen points is necessary for a Championship. A Weimaraner must have at least two major wins (that is, wins of three, four or five points) as part of the fifteen points.

For example, at a show in the state of Virginia the following is the point scale for Weimaraners:

	1 pt		2 pts		3 pts		4 pts		5 pts	
	Male/Female		M	F	M	F	M	F	M	F
Number of dogs and bitches competing	2	2	5	6	9	11	13	15	20	21

In contrast, in a less populated area, with fewer shows the point scale is quite different. For example, at a show held in Wyoming, in the western part of the U.S.A., the scale for 1990-1991 was:

	1 pt		2 pts		3 pts		4 pts		5 pts	
	Male/Female		M	F	M	F	M	F	M	F
Number of dogs and bitches competing	2	2	4	4	6	7	8	9	11	14

Each year the American Kennel Club revises the scale of points for each breed depending upon such factors as: the number of shows obtaining major points, number of Championships awarded, number of total dogs in competition, and a variety of other influencing factors.

FIELD

National Amateur Field Champion Egon Blitzkrieg von Horn CD, Sd, NRD, V.

FIELD CHAMPION (FCH)

Just as a bench Championship is attained by accumulating a required number of points, a similar system governs Field Championships. A Weimaraner must amass a total of ten points which can only be won by being placed first in regular Field Trial Stakes. The number of points is determined by the number of starters:

Number of Starters	Number of points
4 to 7	1
8 to 12	2
13 to 17	3
18 to 24	4
25 or more	5

The dog must have at least one major win (3 points or more) and must have points from at least three different field trials. In addition, a Weimaraner must have a Water Certification (passed a test to demonstrate a water retrieve) or have a Retrieving Dog

OTCh Brought-Mars Samantha P SMOG, TDX, SDX, RDX, VX: The first Obedience Trial Champion in the U.S.A.

(R.D.) or Retrieving Dog Excellent (R.D.X.) rating from the Weimaraner Club of America.

AMATEUR FIELD CHAMPION (AFCH)

The Amateur Field Championship also requires ten points, but, depending on the number of starters, points may be given for first, second or third place. As with the Field Championship, there is a requirement for a Water Certification and a major win.

	Placement		
Number of starters	1st	2nd	3rd
4 to 7	1 point		
8 to 12	2 points		
13 to 17	3 points	1 pt	
18 to 24	4 points	2 pts	
25 or more	5 points	3 pts	1 pt

HUNTING TEST

JUNIOR HUNTER (JH)
SENIOR HUNTER (SH)
MASTER HUNTER (MH)

The American Kennel Club Hunting Test, at which a JH, SH and MH may be earned, is an opportunity for a dog to demonstrate ability to perform in a manner consistent with the demands of actual hunting conditions. The Hunting Test is designed to measure natural abilities and training and is open to all A.K.C. registered Pointing Breeds (Brittanys, German Shorthaired Pointers, German Wirehaired Pointers, English, Irish, Gordon Setters, Vizslas, Weimaraners, and Wirehaired Pointing Griffons). Dogs are judged on a point system, but only a pass or fail is recorded by the A.K.C. Dogs are judged against a standard of performance and not against each other. Four passing scores must be obtained for each Hunting title before the title is conferred.

OBEDIENCE TRIALS

OBEDIENCE (CD)
COMPANION DOG EXCELLENT (CDX)
UTILITY DOG (UD)
OBEDIENCE TRIAL CHAMPION(OTCh)
TRACKING DOG (TD)
TRACKING DOG EXCELLENT (TDX)

Three basic obedience titles are available to the American Weimaraner: Companion Dog (CD); Companion Dog Excellent (CDX); and Utility Dog (UD). The exercises are progressively more difficult and require increased skill on the part of both dog and trainer. Each title is prerequisite for moving on to the next one, so once a dog earns a title of a higher degree of difficulty, the lower title is dropped and the higher one is used. For example, if a dog is shown as having a UD, it is understood that the dog has already earned a CD and CDX. The CD dog must enter the Novice Class, the CDX dog competes in the Open Class, and UD dogs compete in Utility. The exercises are scored on a 200 point scale and 170 points are needed to pass. To earn any title the dog must have three passing scores (170 points or more).

The CD requires: Heeling (on and off lead); a stand for examination; a sit and down exercise while the handler waits across the ring from the dog; and a Recall in which the dog is left in a sitting position on one side of the ring, is called by the handler on the signal of the judge, must sit close in front of the handler and come to a heeling position at the handler's side on the signal of the judge. The CDX builds on the basic skills of the CD, and adds: Heeling totally off lead; retrieving dumb-bell; retrieving dumb-bell over a solid high jump; the Recall exercise with the added feature of being signalled to do a down halfway across the ring before completing the rest of the recall; and doing a broad jump over a series of low wooden hurdles. The sit and down are longer, and the handler leaves the ring and must remain out of sight until the judge orders his or her return. Utility is still more complex with a series of hand signals, scent discrimination where the dog must select both a leather and a metal dumb-bell from among several, of which only one has its owner's scent on it, retrieving one of three gloves at the direction of the handler, and taking hand signal directions to jump either a solid or a bar jump.

OBEDIENCE TRIAL CHAMPION (OTCh)

Only dogs who have attained the title of Utility Dog (UD) may compete for this difficult and coveted obedience title. Points are awarded on the basis of winning first or second place in the Open or Utility classes. One hundred points are needed for the title of OTCh. The number of points awarded is affected by the number of dogs competing. For example, if there are between ten and fourteen dogs competing in a Utility Class, a first place win would give the dog six OTCh points while a second place would merit two points.

In most Obedience Trials dogs of all breeds compete. Dogs who have earned an OTCh may continue to compete in classes with those who have not won OTCh. This makes competition very keen. In the U.S.A. to date, there are only four Weimaraners who have ever attained this title.

OTCh Haiku Solar Eclipse UDT: The first and to date, the only male Weimaraner Obedience Trial Champion.

TRACKING

TRACKING DOG (TD)
TRACKING DOG EXCELLENT (TDX)

Both titles require the dog to follow a track which has been laid by a person that the dog does not know. The track will make turns, cross obstacles such as roadways, low walls etc. The difficulty of the course and its length differentiate the two titles. The angles of the turns in the track, the outside influence of a second track crossing the original track, the nature of the terrain and the length of track are all factors. In order to participate in a Tracking Test the dog must first qualify by doing a track and being certified as being ready to be tested.

WEIMARANER CLUB OF AMERICA TITLES AND EVENTS

FUTURITY AND MATURITY COMPETITIONS

Information about the accomplishments of American Weimaraners may make references to being Futurity/Maturity winner or placer. The Futurity is a national puppy competition, and its purpose is to encourage breeders to give prime consideration to improving the breed in planning their breeding programme.

When a mating is to take place, a member of the WCA may nominate the breeding for inclusion in the Futurity/Maturity programme by recording the mating with the WCA and paying a nomination fee. When the puppies are born, the individual puppies may be kept active in the programme with an additional nomination and payment of a fee (termed a forfeit). Four shows are held each year in which the Futurity-eligible young Weimaraner may compete.

The shows are sponsored by local Weimaraner Clubs and the locations are divided geographically, with an eastern, southern, central and western Futurity. The forfeits form the basis of the prize money awarded at these competitions. There are separate classes for dogs and bitches, and there are three age delineations for the competing puppies: Junior, Intermediate, and Senior. When a Futurity is judged, four placements are made for each of the three classes. The first-place winners compete for Best Dog in Futurity. The bitches are then judged in the same way and a Best Bitch in Futurity is chosen. The Best Dog and Best Bitch then compete for Best in Futurity and for Best of Opposite Sex to Best in Futurity.   The Maturity programme gives an opportunity to the Futurity-eligible puppies to compete the following year as mature dogs and bitches. Maturities are judged at the same show as Futurities and the same judge is used for both competitions. Classes are divided by sex only, and the Best Dog and Best Bitch in Maturity are selected.

BREED REGISTER OF MERIT (BROM)

The WCA BROM is designed to recognise sires and dams that produce top-class offspring. It is the point system in which the offspring accumulate points for their accomplishments in show, field, obedience and tracking competitions. To have the title of BROM confirmed there is an eligibility criterion: sires must have 100 points earned by ten or more progeny, of which eight or more must be Champions; dams must have 50 points earned by five or more progeny, of which four must be Champions. Points are awarded for wins at dog shows, earning a Championship, WCA Futurity wins and obedience titles.

VERSATILITY TITLES AND FIELD ACCOMPLISHMENTS

NOVICE SHOOTING DOG (NSD)
SHOOTING DOG (SD)
SHOOTING DOG EXCELLENT (SDX)

The NSD, SD and SDX tests are designed to test the aptitude of the Weimaraner for hunting, pointing and upland bird field-work. Each title has progressively more difficult requirements. For example, the NSD is used to determine if a young or inexperienced Weimaraner has basic hunting aptitudes. In this test the Weimaraner must demonstrate a desire to hunt, boldness, initiative, ability to indicate the presence of game and reasonable obedience to the handler's commands. Dogs are run in braces for fifteen minutes, and the dog is given the opportunity to indicate the presence of game. The SD requires that the dog has definite hunting ability, bird sense, and some field training. Dogs are run in braces for twenty minutes and must point, but not necessarily be steady to wing and shot. The SDX is a thirty-minute test requiring a dog to be steady on point to wing and shot. A dog encountering its brace-mate on point must honour the point, and the SDX requires retrieving the shot bird. Dogs attaining the rating of SDX must show the class and style expected of top field Weimaraners.

RETRIEVING

> NOVICE RETRIEVING DOG (NRD)
> RETRIEVING DOG (RD)
> RETRIEVING DOG EXCELLENT (RDX)

The same progression for the WCA's Shooting Ratings is found in three retrieving ratings: NRD, RD, RDX. For the NRD the Weimaraner must do a land retrieve of a bird which is a minimum of twenty yards and a maximum of forty yards. A five-minute time frame is allowed for locating the bird and retrieving it to the handler. The NRD water retrieve has the same distance and time requirements. The dog is not required to be steady on the line until released by the handler, and it may be restrained by holding or leashing the dog. The RD requires that the dog is steady on the line until released by the handler.

Both land and water require that two birds are retrieved and the dogs may have up to ten minutes to complete the task. Both land and water require that the birds are wide-spaced (approximate angle of sixty degrees) with the first bird at approximately fifty yards and the second at twenty yards. The water retrieve is through eight decoys. The RDX requires demonstration of obedience, eagerness, and style in a land, water and blind retrieve. The land is a double retrieve at sixty and thirty yards that must be completed within ten minutes. The water is a triple with the first fall at forty yards, the second a minimum of sixty yards through decoys, and the third at twenty yards, landing to the opposite side of the first fall. The time requirement for the triple water retrieve is fifteen minutes. For the RDX title a blind retrieve must also be completed. The dog is brought to the shoreline without seeing where the bird has downed. The handler is advised of the direction and the dog is sent to the location which must be at least fifty yards, through eight decoys. The retrieve must be completed within ten minutes.

VERSATILE EXCELLENT (VX)

Weimaraner owners take great pride in the fact that the breed is known for its versatility in show, field, obedience and tracking accomplishments. To recognise their versatility the WCA offers two titles for the dogs who have sufficiently varied achievements to be deemed versatile, i.e. having advanced titles in three of the following five categories: show, obedience, field, retrieving and tracking. A total of six points is the minimum for a Versatile rating (V), and nine are needed for a

Versatile Excellent (VX). At Weimaraner Speciality Shows the host club may offer a dog show class in which only Weimaraners with a 'V' or 'VX' may be entered.

Points are awarded on the following schedule:

Show 'V' points
Bench Champion 4 points
Ten Bench points (including a major win) 3 points
Five Bench points 2 points
Bench Pointed 1 point

Obedience
Obedience Trial Champion 5 points
Utility Dog (UD) 3 points
Companion Dog Excellent (CDX) 2 points
Companion Dog (CD) 1 point

Field
Field Champion 5 points
Master Hunter 4 points
Senior Hunter or Shooting Dog Excellent (SDX) 3 points
Junior Hunter or Shooting Dog (SD) 2 points
Novice Shooting Dog (NSD) 1 point

Retrieving
Retrieving Dog Excellent (RDX) 3 points
Retrieving Dog (RD) 2 points
Novice Retrieving Dog (NRD) 1 point

Tracking
Tracking Dog Excellent (TDX) 3 points
Tracking Dog (TD) 2 points

Sherry and two grouse, a representative from the Kilborn kennels.

Chapter Fourteen

THE WEIMARANER IN SCANDINAVIA

SWEDEN

The first Weimaraner was imported to Sweden in the early sixties as a pet, rather than as a hunting dog. By 1990 the number of Weimaraners in Sweden had increased to about a hundred, most of which are home-bred. Great emphasis is placed on the hunting ability of dogs, and more and more are being purchased by hunters.

There are strict guidelines relating to the breed, and in Sweden and Norway it has been illegal to dock Weimaraners for the last two years, except for medical reasons. Puppies cannot be registered if the hip scores of the parents are not known, and this rule also applies to imported Weimaraners. All Swedish Champions belonging to the continental pointing breeds have to be cleared from hip dysplasia in order to obtain their titles. A Swedish Show Champion from the gundog breeds also has to win a prize at a Field Trial before getting its title. A Nordic (NordUCH) Show Champion is a dog who is a Champion in Finland, Norway and Sweden. The most successful

SUCH Mymylan: The first Swedish Champion.

SV 89 Faltherrens Wolfram won his title at the Swedish kennel Club's 100th Anniversary Show.

SUCH Malarens Boy: a successful competitor in the Swedish Bloodtrack Championships.

Weimaraners in the last ten years are: SUCH Mymlan, the first Swedish Champion, and her son NordUCH and SUCH Malarens Boy. Boy competed successfully in the Swedish Bloodtrack Championships (DSchweisshundprufung) for all breeds. Other hunting Weimaraners are Mymlan's brother, Mattis, and Boy's brother, Malarens Purdey. Purdey is one of the most useful blood trackers, finding traffic-wounded elk and deer. In the show ring, Arimis, SV 89 Faltherren Wolfram made his name when winning his title at the Swedish Kennel Club's 100 Year Anniversary show.

Weimaraners have proved successful in Obedience Trials. The first Obedience Champion was SLCH SLCH E Rhannigal Ghostbuster. As working dogs, Swedish Weimaraners are known as good trackers and sleigh-pullers. The most successful sleighdogs include: SBCH Drag Faltherrens Canus Ericius, SBCH Drag Myra and Malarens Timmy. The leading Weimaraner kennels in Sweden are Flatherrens Kennel, owned by Lars Kilborn, Malarens, Disodils and Husvargens.

DENMARK

The Danish Weimaraner Club was formed in 1961, and today it has a membership of one hundred and forty, made up from five regions around the country. The club holds three shows a year which usually attract between fifteen and twenty entries. There are also five other shows held under the auspices of the Danish Kennel Club, which attract an average of ten Weimaraners. From 1963 to 1990 a total of one hundred and fifty Weimaraner litters have been registered with the Danish Kennel Club. The Danish Kennel Club also organise a Field Trial every year in April, a gundog retrieving test, and Schweiss Trials, which is a tracking test using a blood scent.

NORWAY

There are some eighty Weimaraners in Norway, and only a few of these are used for hunting. They are entered for Schweiss Trials, as in Denmark. One of Norway's most successful Weimaraners is the bitch, Ferra Die Graue, bred by Lene Borud of Trogstad, the result of a mating between Blitz von der Steinhorst and Dana von der Walelburg – both German imports. This bitch was entered for a hunting test at only seven months old and was the best of the young dogs, and in the spring and summer she is used in Schweiss Trials, where she is the only Weimaraner in Norway to have won a First. She is a dual-purpose dog and has won honours in the show ring in both Norway and Sweden, including Best of Breed and Best Bitch at the Norwegian Kennel Club Shows. Ferra has also competed in Obedience Trials, where Weimaraners have a good record of success.

Ferra's owner, Eva Eriksen, also owns a younger Weimaraner, Faltherrens Venus, who was born in 1989. At the Norwegian Kennel Club Show in December 1990 this bitch went Best Youngster and reserve Best Bitch in Breed. She was bred by Agneta and Lars Kilborn in Sweden. She is also dual-purpose, and she is used for hunting in woods, mountain and water. In 1990 she received a first prize in a hunting test in

ABOVE: Ferra die Graue, owned by Eva Eriksen, is one of Norway's most successful Weimaraners, winning honours in the show ring, in obedience trials and in the field.

LEFT: Top Norweigian winner Felix Gracilis, the only Weimaraner to win a hunting test in woodland.

Faltherrens Venus: Best Youngster and Reserve Best Bitch in Breed at the Norweigian Kennel Club Show in 1990. In the same year she also received first prize in a hunting test.

retrieving, and was best young dog of all the breeds in that test. The top Norwegian winner in 1989 was Felix Gracilis, bred by Lene Borud and owned by Egil Salthammer/Kari Kjorholt of Notodden, Norway. Felix is brother to Ferra Die Graue, and has won a hunting test in woodland – the only Weimaraner to have done this. These dogs come from German lines and seem to be proving both good working and good show dogs.

Chapter Fifteen

BREEDING

THE BROOD BITCH

A brood bitch is the most important component of a kennel. She is the blueprint of your breeding stock, and she must possess all the attributes which enable her to produce a line of dogs which is distinctive in type. Above all, she must be sound in both temperament and physique, for she is the foundation of your stock. No bitch is perfect, but she must conform to the Breed Standard in all its essentials.

Ideally, she should not have any white colouring. A small white patch on the chest is permissible, but most breeders try to eliminate this, and I have now bred several generations of pale silver dogs without any white colouring. The bitch must be healthy and free from any hereditary defects, such as entropion. Any defect will almost certainly be passed on to her offspring, perhaps not in the first litter, but it is likely to arise in subsequent litters. It is not fair on your customers to breed puppies knowing full well that there is a defect in the parents; it is obviously bad for the breed, but it will also reflect badly on your kennel. A brood bitch should be kept in peak condition, neither too fat nor too thin, and you should keep a check on her seasons. Most Weimaraner bitches come into season twice-yearly; however, I known some that come in every four months. As long as the seasons are normal (approximately three weeks in duration) and regular, there is no cause for concern. If the bitch has had any medication such as hormone treatment which may affect her seasons, it is advisable to wait until she has had one normal season before trying to mate her. The bitch must have a sound temperament. A nervous Weimaraner should never be bred from, as this disposition can be passed on to the offspring. She will also have to put up with a lot of visitors when she has her puppies, and she must be prepared to accept the intrusion.

So, take a good, hard look at your bitch before you decide whether to breed from her. Of course, you think she is wonderful, and the idea of a beautiful litter of Weimaraner puppies is tempting, but breeding and rearing a litter is hard work, and it is a big responsibility. A great deal of thought has to go into it. You will need to find homes for all the puppies that you do not intend to keep, and these must be suitable, caring homes. The new owners will telephone you with all kinds of enquiries, and you must be suitably qualified – and have the time – to answer them. You must also be prepared to rehouse any pups which 'bounce', failing to find a suitable home first time round. An established kennel will receive enquiries for puppies all the time, especially if the stock is good. But however great the demand, do not try to over-breed. It is not desirable to breed from a bitch that is either too young or too old. Puppies cannot be registered from a bitch over eight years, and no bitch should have a litter more than once a year. It is easy to think that breeding is a profitable business, but there are a lot of expenses to take into account before you actually make any money. Breeders must always have the welfare of the breed at heart. If you fail to do this, it is your stock and your kennel which will suffer in the long run. There is no short cut to breeding sound, healthy stock.

When you have finally decided to breed a litter, you must try to make a critical assessment of your bitch in order to discover what areas could be improved upon. Are her ears too short? Is she too short in the back? Would you like to improve her head, or her feet? Once you recognise the faults of your bitch, you can start to look for a male which is strong in the areas that needs improvement, and one that will complement your bitch in terms of bloodlines and type. This is not an easy task. You will find everyone is very friendly when they know you have a bitch of mateable age, but take care! A friendly and helpful person does not necessarily have the dog that will suit your bitch. You may have to travel a long way to find the right mate, but it is worth it in the end. It is very tempting – and very convenient – to use your own dogs on your own bitches, but this can only be done for a short period before a new dog is needed to revitalise bloodlines. When a new dog with completely

A brood bitch for the Beckstone Weimaraners: Beckstone Adriana, aged six months.
Dalton

Beckstone Fenmaiden of Trilite (Four Green stars) and a foundation bitch in Ireland.

different bloodlines – an outcross – has been introduced, the resulting offspring can be put back to your own lines. Breeding can take place between relatives such as cousin to cousin, nephew to aunt, grandson to grand-dam, grand-sire to grand-daughter and uncle to niece, and this is known as line breeding. It can only be successful if the lines are sound, because any hereditary defects are certain to be reproduced. However, if the lines are very sound, then the stock can only improve. If a defect arises after several generations of line breeding and then using an outcross, it will almost certainly be the new dog that is to blame. A kennel that wants to keep its type and line must line-breed. It is impossible to keep a type by

Sh. Ch. Hansom Hirondelle: dam of six Show Champions. Bred by R. M. W. Finch. owned by Denise Mosey.

outcrossing continually. In-breeding is totally different. This is when close relatives are mated, i.e. father to daughter, or son to mother. This is very 'close' breeding, and both parties have to be extremely sound in the body and temperament. However, it is not wise to become too tightly related in bloodlines, especially if you are seeking improvement. Do not fall into the danger of becoming kennel-blind, failing see the faults in your own stock. Every dog is special to its owner, but it is up to the breeders to improve the breed, and they are responsible for the Weimaraners of tomorrow.

Information on dogs that are standing at stud can be found in year books, which can be obtained from breed clubs. It is a good idea to visit the stud dog before making a final decision. Has he got the improved physical characteristics that you require? Has he been hip-scored and eye-tested? Has he had any operations or other medical history that is relevant? It is vital that you know all the facts, as you can pay as high a stud fee for an unsound dog as for a sound one – so make plenty of

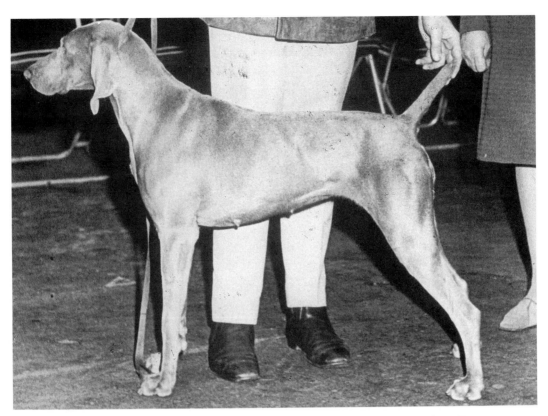

Sh. Ch. Hansom Hobby Hawk: The first Weimaraner to win a Gundog Group at an All breeds Championship Show, and dam of many winning offspring. Owned and bred by Mr. R. M. W. Finch.

enquiries and study plenty of pedigrees. If you are embarking on breeding your first litter, it is worth going back to your bitch's breeder. There is no substitute for experience, and you will probably be able to pick up some valuable advice. There are no short-cuts when you are planning a suitable mating, so give yourself plenty of time to find a suitable mate. The best time to start is when the bitch comes into season, prior to the season when you want to mate her.

The bitch you are planning to breed with should be in good condition, and before she comes into season you should check that her inoculations are up to date, and she should be wormed. When the bitch has come in heat, the next step is to inform the stud dog owner to arrange a convenient time to visit. Ideally, your bitch should be mated twice, on separate occasions, but if you are travelling a long distance this may not be possible. Some stud dog owners will accommodate you overnight so your bitch can have a second mating the following day. This also gives you time to get to know the dog and owner and chat about the breed. Make sure you have agreed on a

Father and son: Sh. Ch. Gunalt Carcharel, winner of 17 CCs and twelve-week-old
Gunalt Farenheit.   *Keith Allison*

stud fee before the mating: it might be more than you expected and this precaution could save some embarrassment. You may also negotiate a deal, such as a puppy in exchange for the stud fee, but this should all be signed and sealed before the mating. Remember to take your bitch's pedigree with you, unless you have already exchanged pedigrees with the stud keeper.

A bitch's season lasts for three weeks and most are ready for mating between the eleventh and the fifteenth day. However, some bitches may vary, and so if you are in any doubt it is best to have your bitch swab-tested by the vet. This will tell you when she is ready, which is a great help, particularly if you are travelling a long distance. The biggest single problem for newcomers to breeding is to detect the first day a bitch comes into season. A bitch will usually lick herself a lot, and the vulva will look slightly larger than normal. There will be a milky-coloured discharge, which soon becomes a bloody discharge. The first day of bleeding should be counted as the first day of the season. Most of my bitches are ready for mating on the twelfth and fourteenth day, but I have also had one who was ready on her tenth day. The signs to look for are when the discharge changes to a pinkish colour, and if you rub your hand along her back she will probably put her tail to one side, indicating that she is ready to stand. If you own a dog yourself, he will tell you by howling, and she will respond. You must make sure that your bitch is kept secure from other dogs on the premises when she is in season. If your bitch does get mis-mated then you should take her to the vet straightaway, and she can be injected against having a litter. There is no point in going to all the trouble of rearing a litter if the parents are incompatible. Most bitches are mated twice, and if a bitch fails to come into whelp the stud owner will probably offer a free return mating. However, the stud fee must be paid on the first visit, and the size of the fee will vary according to the sire's success in the breeding paddocks.

THE STUD DOG

If you own a dog and you are contemplating putting him out to stud, you must consider the pitfalls. A stud dog always gets the blame if anything goes wrong – the bitch's part in the proceedings is largely forgotten. If the puppies are ugly – your dog threw them. If there are any health problems – your dog is responsible. In order to keep a stud dog you should have reasonable experience of dog management, and you should be aware of the commitment you are making in terms of time. Brood bitches and their owners can arrive at any time of the day if they are travelling a considerable distance, and they may stay quite a while if the bitch is not immediately receptive. So think hard before advertising your dog for stud duties.

Ch. Ragstone Ryuhlan J.W. and winner of 15 CCs, a sire that has appeared in many pedigrees. Owned and bred by Mrs G. W. Burgoin.

From the breeding point of view, your dog must be sound – and that does not just mean that he is able to run up the field and back. He must conform to the Breed Standard, he must be free from any hereditary defects, and his medical record should stand up to scrutiny, with no evidence of corrective surgery. The dog must not be over-sized or under-sized, and he should be eye-tested and hip-scored. This is an expensive business, but it is well worth it. It is no good mating a bitch with a low hip score to a dog with a high score. The lower the overall score, the better chance you have of producing sound offspring. Of course, there is no guarantee that your dog will not throw offspring with this problem, for it may exist somewhere in his pedigree a few generations back, but the responsible breeder should take all reasonable precautions. I think it is essential that all Weimaraners used for breeding are eye-tested, as conditions such as entropion are very prevalent in the breed today. If your dog has any defects, he should not be used at stud.

Finally, the temperament of your dog is an important consideration. He must not show any vicious tendencies, and he should be easy to manage and obedient. When he is asked to mate a bitch he will become highly excitable, so he has to be controlled, and accept that you are in charge of proceedings. It is amazing the change that comes over some dogs when a bitch in season arrives on the premises. One minute a dog can be lounging on the sofa without a care in the world, and then

Sh. Ch. Hansom Brandyman of Gunalt: Winner of 19 CCs and a top sire in the breed. Owned by Mr and Mrs S. A. Hollings. Bred by Mr R. M. W. Finch.   Dave Freeman

suddenly he is leaping around like a mad March hare! Obviously, you want a dog that is keen, but control and good management are the key to successful stud work.

THE MATING

The dog and bitch must be given time to get to know each other before the mating takes place. To begin with, the bitch may not be too friendly, and she may need encouragement to help her to settle. It is important to have someone that is experienced in stud work in charge of the proceedings, for things do not always go according to plan. It is also important that any other dogs or bitches on the premises are kept well away.

When the bitch has got used to the dog, he will try and mount her. She may respond by spinning round and trying to play, so don't try and rush them. Both the dog and the bitch should be on leads, so that they are under control. As the dog mounts the bitch, the owner of the bitch should hold her head to steady her and prevent her from jumping about too much. However, she should not be forced, or held too tightly. The dog will try and mount the bitch several times; it can take as long as fifteen minutes before he is properly engaged. It is vital that the bitch is held steady until the dog is ready to turn. He may need some help to accomplish this move, but he should end up facing the opposite direction to the bitch. The pair are now tied, and the stud owner will probably hold them in place until they part. This is to prevent the bitch from pulling away, which could injure the dog. The tie can last from ten minutes to sixty minutes – so be prepared for a long session. The dog and bitch should never be left unsupervised at this stage.

When the tie is completed and the dog 'falls out', the bitch should be taken away and allowed to rest in the car or in a kennel. The stud owner will then check the dog. This is to make sure that the dog's penis has returned to its sheath. This does not usually cause a problem, but if it is very dry it may fail to do so, and in this instance a vet will be needed to assist. The whole mating procedure should be repeated in a day or two, and then the bitch should be allowed to follow her normal routine. If a bitch takes an absolute dislike to the dog and fails to co-operate, this is probably because she is not ready and she should be tried again later on in her season. If she still resists the male's advances, consult your vet, as there may be some underlying problem. However, I have generally found that Weimaraners are an easy breed to handle in this situation, and most will be only too happy to oblige.

Chapter Sixteen

WHELPING

Most Weimaraner bitches make excellent mothers. They love the extra attention they get when they are in whelp and while they are rearing their offspring. However, the bitch must have a good temperament to start with. Weimaraner bitches usually become very close to their owners when they are in whelp, and as an owner, you must be prepared to give extra fuss and reassurance over this stressful period. Weimaraners usually have an average of eight puppies in a litter. Some bitches tend to have larger litters – one of my bitches once had thirteen puppies. If this happens, it is advisable to cull some of the pups. A large litter can put too much strain on the bitch, and the quality of the puppies will be affected. This is always a difficult decision to make, but the welfare of the bitch must be of paramount importance.

The period after mating and before the puppies are due is the time to get yourself organised. There is no point waiting until the bitch is ready to whelp and then deciding that the kitchen is an unsuitable place for the birth. The bitch will require somewhere that is peaceful with limited distractions. She has a hard job ahead of her, and she will cope much better if she is comfortable and feels secure. In most households the kitchen is the centre of activity, and so it is probably the worst place for your bitch to be. Equally, you may not wish to share your mealtimes with a litter of puppies, so give the matter some thought.

After your bitch has been mated, she should be kept in good condition. She will not require any extra food until she is approximately five weeks in whelp. If you feed her extra rations too soon she will become overweight, and whelping will be harder for her. At five weeks she will require two meals a day, and these should be fed at regular times. There are many feeds on the market that are specifically designed for brood bitches, and they are very good. Follow the manufacture's instructions, and don't over-feed. Make sure she is well-covered, but not fat. If you introduce a change of diet, make sure you do this gradually so that her digestion is not upset. Some brood bitch diets contain extra calcium, but if they do not you should supplement the feed with one calcium tablet a day. This is in order to reduce the risk of a calcium deficiency, which could lead to eclampsia – a potentially fatal condition. Fresh water should be available at all times.

A bitch in whelp still needs exercise, and she will enjoy a daily walk. However, do not allow her to romp about, especially with other dogs, in the latter weeks of her pregnancy. This could lead to a rise in her temperature, which would not do her any good, quite apart from any damage she could inflict on the unborn puppies. You will need to buy or build a whelping box for the bitch to use when she delivers her puppies and for rearing. It must be solid in substance and sit firmly on the floor. They are usually made from wood, and this can be obtained secondhand to reduce the cost. However, the wood must be clean, free from any splinters and easy to wash out. The whelping box must be big enough to accommodate the bitch comfortably so she can move around freely. I suggest that it should be 40ins. x 40ins. in size, and the walls should be 6ins. in height. This takes up quite a lot of space, so make sure it is well out of the way of human comings and goings. Running around the top of the box you should install a rail, approximately 7ins. wide, to prevent the bitch squashing her whelps against the sides of the box. The rail can be removed when the puppies are three weeks old. It is useful to fit hinges to one side of the box, and this can be let down when the puppies get bigger and start to move about. The bitch should get used to her whelping quarters and her whelping box a few days before the litter is due. Left to herself, she would probably have her puppies on your bed or in the airing cupboard, so make sure she knows where she is expected to be, and that she is happy with the arrangement. Try and find a quiet corner of the house to put her in; the spare room, or a utility room may be suitable, or even the garden shed if it is big enough. You will need a heat-lamp of some kind – pig lamps are cheap and easily available, and they are safe. I prefer to use white bulbs. This lamp can be fixed over the whelping box and adjusted when the bitch is settled. Do not have the room too hot, as this will make the bitch uncomfortable. The ideal temperature is 65 degrees Fahrenheit. Whelping is a messy business, and the whelping box should be lined with plenty of newspaper, or shredded bedding. This is a good product, but don't use too much or you will lose the pups in it. I find the best bedding for whelping down is old, clean electric blankets, with the wires removed. These can be purchased from dog shows or dog papers, and they are like blotting paper. When your bitch has finished whelping the bedding needs to be disposed of, and fresh blankets or a product such as Vetbed can be used.

As the day of delivery draws nearer you will notice your bitch becoming more restless. She will now resemble a nanny goat rather than a Weimaraner. Her milk glands will be becoming full, and she will start to 'drop'. This is when the pups become engaged and her whole body seems to get lower to the ground. At the back of her ribs you may be able to see a hollow; this usually happens about a week before the bitch delivers. Some bitches are so full there is not much change in overall shape, but the majority do 'drop'. The pregnancy lasts for an average of sixty-three days, and the bitch may start digging up her bed in readiness, sometimes as much as a week in advance. However, you must always be prepared, for pups can arrive as much as a week earlier than expected. This happened to one of my bitches and surprised us all! The puppies will come when they are ready, and the only cause for concern is if the bitch goes seven days beyond her whelping date, or if she goes into labour and fails to produce a pup.

On the day your bitch whelps you will probably see a marked change in her character. She will become more reserved, and she may leave her food. Keep an eye on her, especially when you let her outside, as you don't want her disappearing and having her puppies in a distant field. Hopefully, she will settle in her box, and as the birth approaches she will start to make a nest. The first stage can take up to twelve hours. You will need to be on hand to assist the bitch, and so make sure you are dressed suitably. As the delivery progresses your bitch will start to strain. She may turn around in her box, lie down, and then start fidgeting about. The labour will progress at its own speed; she will not change her mind once she has started, unless she has difficulty in producing a pup. You will need a watch, and a pad and pen so that you can note the times when each pup is born. There may be half an hour between deliveries, or sometimes an hour. Contractions should become stronger as each pup is delivered, but you will be in for a long session – and most bitches whelp at night.

As each pup is expelled it appears in a dark greenish-coloured sac. Sometimes a pup will be born without a sac; if so, it should be expelled soon after the pup has 'dropped'. Leave the bitch to deal with each pup. Instinct will show her what to do:

she will eat each sac as the puppy is expelled from it – this will look awful but it is important she does. The sacs contain nutriments and will sustain her during this hard time. She will then bite through each cord which attaches the puppy to the bitch. The end of the cord attached to the puppy will shrivel up in a few days and fall off. If the bitch is coping with biting the cord, leave well alone. However, if she fails to break the cord – and this is rare – you will have to cut it. This is done by tying the cord with a small strand of string, at the puppy's end. Then cut the cord, approximately four inches away from where it is tied. The string can be removed about an hour later. It is useful to have a few strands of string and a pair of disinfected scissors ready, just in case. All the equipment you need for whelping should be readily available, as this can save a mad panic when the bitch has started to whelp. Sometimes a sac is tough and hard to break. In this instance you may need to intervene and break the sac near the nose of the puppy, so it can breath. If you find that the puppy is not attempting to move, give it a firm rub up and down its body until it squeaks; it will then start to breath. You may have to repeat the sequence several times. If after five minutes the puppy is still lifeless, then it is best to leave it alone. If the bitch expels a dead puppy you will have to remove it from the bitch. You will probably find that if a puppy is born lifeless the bitch will ignore it. This is nature's way. Before each puppy is born, move the existing puppies to one corner of the whelping box; this will stop the bitch treading on them. Do not forget, she is still at work. When she has had two or three puppies she may rest. It is then you can place each puppy to feed. The earlier they feed, the better; but don't try to force the bitch – she will probably be reluctant to lie still for very long.

As soon as the puppies are born, their noses will change from a grey colour to a bright pink colour. Observe the noses when checking your puppies as any change in colour could give notice of a cold puppy, or one that is unwell. If you are going to lose a pup, it is usually within the first forty-eight hours, but at this early stage there is little you can do, except make sure the litter is kept warm. Record the time that each puppy is born and its sex, and then you will know exactly what you have at the end of whelping, without disturbing the nest too much. This is also helpful if you have to call the vet, as he will want to know when the last pup was born. It is important to make a note of the time that the bitch starts pushing. If she has been pushing and straining for forty-five minutes and has still failed to produce a puppy, you should contact your vet. It may be that a whelp has got stuck, and if the bitch continues to strain she will become exhausted. Some breeders weigh each puppy, but I never do; you can usually see if puppies are gaining or losing weight. As whelping proceeds you may find there is a longer gap between arrivals. This is probably due to the bitch getting tired, and is no cause for concern; try to leave the process to nature as much as possible. However, if you are concerned about the proceedings, call your vet. Weimaraners generally whelp with little or no problems, but if you are worried, do not delay in seeking advice. If a bitch fails to expel a puppy, or if she is exhausted, or has any other complications, the vet will need to perform a cesarean section. This operation has to be carried out under general anaesthetic at the surgery. Time is vital, in order to save the lives of the puppies, and possibly the bitch. After the operation the bitch will need a great deal of care, and she should be under intensive observation for the first twenty-four hours. The puppies may be sleepy to begin with, as a result of the anaesthetic given to the mother, and they may sleep for a couple of hours. However, it is important that they start suckling before too long a delay. The bitch must be given peace and quiet after the operation, as her hearing will be more acute after the anaesthetic, and if you note any change in her condition, inform the vet at once.

The heat lamp must be kept on at all times, at least until the puppies are three weeks of age. If it is hot weather, the puppies will still require heat at night. When the bitch has finished whelping she will probably want to go outside and pass water, keep an eye on her just in case she passes another pup. If someone else is around, they can take the bitch out, which will give you opportunity to check the puppies. The bitch will soon settle down with her new offspring and begin cleaning them. It is important that the bitch licks the puppies as this stimulates the pups to pass water. When you are confident that the whelping is finished you will need to change the bedding; from now on, the bed must be kept dry. When the bitch goes out again, remove the pups from the bed and nail down the Vetbed – or whatever bedding you are using– to the whelping box. There is no need to go mad with the nails, as you are going to have to remove them at a later date. However, if the bedding is secured it stops the puppies getting trapped underneath when the bitch decides to re-arrange the bed, as they frequently do. It is impossible to be with a litter twenty-four hours a day, and so this is a sensible precaution to take. I remember coming home, after collecting my daughter from school, to find the nice, new bedding rolled up in a ball and inside were three squealing puppies. Since then, I have always nailed down the bedding.

Most puppies will soon get the idea of suckling. If you find one pup is slightly smaller than the others, place it on the bitch a little more often, and it will soon catch up. The bitch should be monitored closely for the first forty-eight hours, and the first week after whelping can be very tiring for all concerned. However, it is well worth it if all the puppies survive and are healthy, and the bitch is fit and well. As each day progresses the pups will grow dramatically. Keep a check on the bitch's milk-flow during this vital time. If there is any hardening around each breast, express a little

The puppies are settled comfortably with the mother, Ferndyke Super Sluth. This litter was bred by Mr and Mrs D. Burton.

milk to relieve the pressure. This can happen if the bitch has a lot of milk; however, if you are concerned, contact your vet. Fresh drinking water should be available at all times for the bitch. For several days after whelping, your bitch will discharge a dark fluid from her vulva, which is completely normal. However, if she starts to strain, there may be an afterbirth left inside her; she will need to see a vet, who will remove it without too much discomfort to the bitch. If the discharge from the bitch becomes smelly or changes in any way, see the vet. The bitch may have an infection; if it is not treated she may lose her milk. The bitch's motions will be very dark in colour for the first day or two; these will soon return to normal when the bitch resumes her normal food. She may not eat too much to start with, as she has eaten all the afterbirths, so offer her a light meal as a beginning.

When the puppies are born they will be striped; this will disappear in a few days and the coat will take on a metallic sheen. At three days of age the puppies will require docking, and dew claws will need to be removed. Both these operations must be carried out by a vet, so do let your vet know when the litter has arrived. Make sure your vet knows exactly the length you require for the tails, as not all vets are familiar with the Breed Standard. In short-coats, the best method is to use a ten-pence piece as a measure. This can be placed under the tail, and the tail should be removed to its edge. It will then be correct length when the dog is fully grown. In long-coats it is customary to remove just the tip of the tail.

Chapter Seventeen

REARING

During the first few weeks after delivery the bitch must be well fed, and her protein levels must be high. A special complete diet can be purchased from all pet shops, and all you need to do is follow the manufacturer's instructions. If you find the bitch is becoming too hot under the heat lamp, you will have to place the lamp a little higher – but make sure the puppies are warm. Check the puppies' nails from two weeks of age onwards; they will need to be trimmed, as they will make the bitch's udders sore if they are too long. At two weeks of age the puppies will start to open their eyes; they will be sapphire blue in colour, and these will slowly change in the coming weeks to a paler colour. The pale silver colour of the coat and the lovely blue eyes of the Weimaraner puppy make it unique – they are exact miniatures of their parents. If the bitch is fed at regular times during her pregnancy and looked after well, her litter should all be even in size; careful handling and keen observation during the early stages can make the difference between a poor litter and a good one.

At approximately three weeks of age, or when your puppies eyes have completely opened, you will be able to start weaning. All breeders have their own ideas on when to wean, and what food to use. This is my method, tried and tested over several

The Ferndyke Super Sluth puppies at three weeks – their eyes have now opened.

years. I like to start weaning as soon as possible, as I believe this gets the puppies off to a good start. It also means that they do not take so much out of the bitch. If the litter is a large one, this is particularly important. Your bitch must be kept in tip-top condition – there is no need for her to look drawn and thin just because she is rearing a litter. If your bitch falls into bad order she will resent the suckling puppies. They will become hungry and this will make weaning more difficult. You will be receiving many visitors over the next few weeks, and both litter and mum should look their best – otherwise it is a poor reflection on you. There are lots of puppy weaning powders on the market, and all are easy to prepare. Use a shallow oval bowl for feeding, and if the puppies are a bit reluctant to feed at first, dip your fingers in the food and let the puppy lick it off your finger, coaxing the puppy nearer the food. They will soon get the hang of it and most puppies are usually feeding from the bowl within a day. Feed twice daily to start with, and after five days you can then increase to three meals a day. When the puppies are about five weeks of age you can take the bitch away from the litter for approximately half an hour before you feed them. Don't let the puppies become too full – they will eat until they can eat no more – so if your puppy looks nice and rounded take the remaining food away. Again, you must feed at regular times. If you feed at any time, and feed too much, the puppies could develop problems such as hernias. When the puppies are six

The puppies should be fed from a shallow oval bowl to begin with.

weeks old you can take the bitch away for approximately an hour before the feed. By this stage she will appreciate a little time to herself. However, do not allow her to rush around and become hot. If her milk becomes too hot, it is dangerous to puppies, so if by any chance, she does become over-heated, keep her separated from the puppies for half an hour, or until she settles. The puppies will have just been fed, so they will not come to any harm. As each week progresses, lengthen the time the bitch spends away from the youngsters, and give the youngsters a little more food. At approximately four to five weeks the puppies will need a change of food. I usually feed Omega Puppy at this stage. Again, there are a wide variety of complete puppy foods available. The puppies should be feeding well, and putting on weight without getting fat. Make sure they do not become 'bound up' (constipated), or at

They can graduate to individual feeding bowls as they get older.

the opposite extreme, that their stools are not too runny. This can happen if a change of diet is introduced too quickly, but if it persists, try another type of food. However, avoid chopping and changing too often – most puppy foods are excellent and cause very little trouble in the majority of puppies.

When the puppies are five weeks old they will be having longer play periods, and they will benefit from having some toys to amuse themselves with. These do not need to be expensive items from a pet shop, anything will do as long as it safe, for the puppies will chew it endlessly. I let them have an old trainer, and they absolutely love it. However, the laces and inner-soles should be removed, as well as the rims around the lace holes before the puppies get to work on it! At this stage the puppies will require worming. The worming treatment, plus advice about administration can be obtained from your vet. You must not worm your bitch when she is feeding puppies; this must wait until the puppies have left. By now you can check the puppies' mouths – they should already have a scissor bite. The ears must also be checked regularly for mites and dirt. It is surprising how dirty puppies' ears can get. By seven weeks the puppies will be quite large, and they will need additional space to play and exercise. A kennel and run is ideal, as this gives the puppies the chance to play or sleep whenever they choose. They are lovely to watch at this age, and they will also benefit from meeting and playing with people. I usually have a continuous

Puppies love to explore, and a run in the garden is the safest way of giving a litter its first taste of the outside world.

stream of youngsters to visit the pups, as my daughter always informs her classmates of our arrivals. This contact does not harm the puppies, or the bitch. They must learn to accept visitors. The bitch should not show any aggression, and she should never be shut away from her offspring when visitors call. Obviously she will keep watch over the puppies, just like any mum, but she has no need to feel threatened. The puppies should not be nervous, and the constant visitors will help the puppies become accustomed to noise. I never have visitors earlier than three weeks, as I like to give the puppies time to get established. By seven weeks the puppies should be completely weaned and not feeding from the bitch at all. If weaning is done gradually, this is a natural transition, and the puppies should settle quickly when they leave the litter to go to their new homes.

The next big decision is when to release your puppies. This should be planned well in advance if you want to advertise the litter for sale. Puppies are usually ready at eight weeks, by which time they should have been wormed twice, and be fully weaned. They should be receiving four meals a day, spaced at regular intervals throughout the day – including a meal last thing at night. They should be drinking a water/milk mix, which should be available at all times. Before selling your puppies it is wise to insure them. This can at least replace the cost of a puppy to its owner if anything unfortunate happens. You should also compile a diet sheet for each puppy for the new owners to take away. The puppies will also need to be registered. When the bitch was mated you should have received a form signed by the the stud dog's owner, and this is your registration form. If you have a kennel name or affix, you can name the puppies with this preceding the puppy's name. Each puppy has to be named and a spare name also has to be submitted, just in case someone else has the name. The fee required is printed on the form, and this, together with the form, has to be sent to the Kennel Club registration department. The process can take up to a couple of months, so post early. Each puppy you sell must be accompanied by a pedigree; you can either have your own printed, or you can obtain printed ones from a pet shop. I have an envelope for each puppy, so that I can keep all the relevant documents together. It is important to point out to all customers that the puppy they are buying is open to all infection, and it must be kept away from other dogs until it has received its inoculations.

Chapter Eighteen

AILMENTS AND HEREDITARY DISORDERS

The Weimaraner is a sound, healthy breed of dog, and with reasonable luck and care, your dog will live to a ripe old age. There are, however, a number of health problems which affect all dogs, and the responsible dog owner should be able to spot the signs in order to take the necessary action.

AILMENTS

WORMS

Worm infestation is the most common ailment in all dogs, and Weimaraners are no exception. They require regular worming throughout their lives. When you first acquire a puppy it should have been wormed, and it is important that you ask the breeder when the puppy was last wormed and how often it has been treated. Your vet is the best person to advise about worming products, and he will be able to supply the correct dosage for your dog. However, it is as bad to over-worm your dog as under-worm it. I once heard of someone who wormed their dog every week! The same person was also very concerned that the dog in question was not doing too well. Worming twice a year, on average, is sufficient – unless your dog has a large infestation. There are several kinds of worms, and the signs of infestation are: a poor coat that lacks gloss, weight loss, and a ravenous appetite. If your dog continues to show these symptoms after careful worming, contact your veterinary surgeon.

ROUNDWORMS (Toxocara Canis): These are also called ascarids, and they are mainly found in puppies and pregnant bitches. They resemble a thin worm or a soggy strand of spaghetti. They can be up to nine inches long and pale in colour. They are caught from dog to dog, either by licking or from faeces. The eggs cannot be seen.

TAPEWORMS (Taenia and Dipylidium species): These are found predominantly in the adult dog; they can be transmitted from rabbits, mice and birds. They are recognisable by their whitish-coloured segments which join together to form a tape. They may also look like wriggling white particles. If you suspect your dog has a large infestation, worm your dog twice in a short period of time. This should eradicate the problem.

FLEAS, LICE AND TICKS

These are the most common ectoparasites – parasites which live on the skin. Weimaraners do not tend to suffer much from fleas as their coats are very short. This also makes it very easy to detect any sign of them. When you brush your dog check for any spots or red marks. This should be done at least once a week. If you are worried, ask your vet and he can supply a spray which should cure the problem. If you own a cat or other dogs, it is important that you treat all the animals.

EAR MITES

Weimaraners can suffer from ear mites; their clear ears, protected by a flap, make an ideal home for ear mites. They can be seen as greyish dots in the ear canal. If the dog persistently shakes its head or scratches its ears, it may be infested. The ears may also contain brown wax. This condition should be detected in the early stages

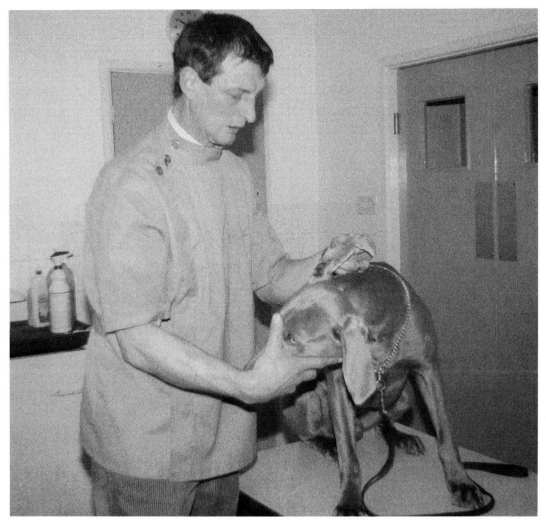

Vet William Oakes checks a Weimaraner's ear for mites.

as blood clots can form in the ear flaps as a result of continuous shaking, and these will need to be removed by surgery. Treatment for ear mites is available from the vet, and the problem should soon be solved. If your Weimaraner is irritable around the ears after a walk, it may have a grass seed down its ear. If you suspect your dog has an ear problem, contact your veterinary surgeon as soon as possible.

BAD BREATH

This can be very unpleasant – there is nothing worse than a dog looking you straight in the face, with breath like rotten fish. The first step is to find out what is causing the problem. It may be due to an infection of the gums or bad teeth. The vet should look at the dog's mouth and check to see whether a small piece of bone or foreign body has stuck in the teeth. If the problem persists, it is worth looking at the dog's diet – the bad breath could be caused by something you are feeding. It may be solved by giving the dog a bone, which will help to clean its teeth. You can also try giving your dog Amplex veterinary tablets, or one of the many natural remedies such as garlic tablets, which are readily available.

BALANITIS

This is quite a common ailment especially in young dogs. It is an infection of the sheath of the penis. The dog will continually lick and clean himself, and he will probably have a thickish white discharge. This can be unpleasant, but generally it is not serious. Consult your vet and he will prescribe an antibiotic.

PYOMETRA

This is a condition that can affect bitches once they have started their seasons. It usually occurs up to nine weeks after a season has finished. The bitch will drink an enormous amount of water, she will be restless, and she may be sick. The bitch's temperature will be higher than normal, and she may clean herself around her vulva a great deal, as though she were in season. She may have a foul smell in the later stages. It is vital that you see a vet as soon as you suspect this condition as she will probably require a hysterectomy. Urgent attention is required, as this condition can prove fatal.

ECLAMPSIA

This is a serious condition which can affect brood bitches of all breeds. It is caused by a shortage of calcium. The first signs are the bitch becomes unsteady on her feet, as though she was drunk. She may also stiffen up, and sometimes the muscles will twitch. An injection of calcium is urgently required, and recovery is usually swift. However, unless prompt action is taken this condition is fatal.

HEREDITARY DISORDERS

All breeds of dog carry hereditary defects, and some conditions are more prevalent in particular breeds. For example, the Weimaraner has shown a tendency towards

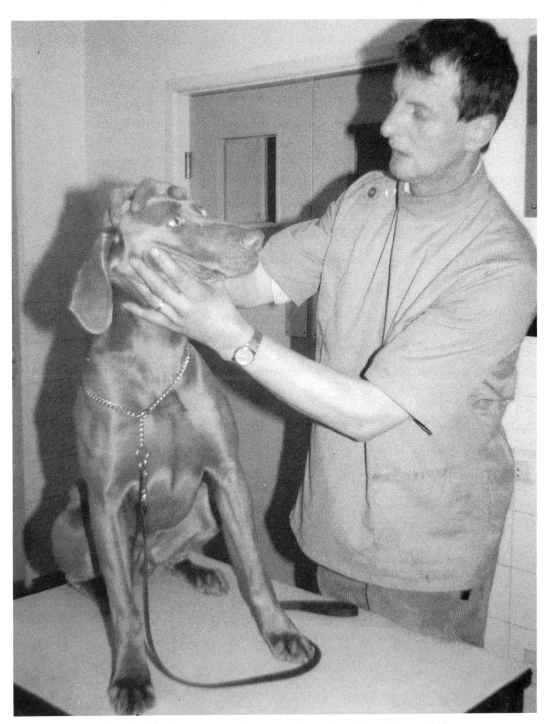

The eyes must be checked to ensure they are clear from hereditary defects.

carrying hereditary eye defects. The incidence of hereditary conditions fluctuates over a period of time, and great care should be taken in any breeding programme to eliminate any of these defects. There is no guarantee that the dogs you produce will be free from hereditary disorders, but you should take all reasonable safeguards. Equally, if you suspect a dog has a hereditary condition, it should not be used for breeding under any circumstances. If you persist in breeding from dogs with these problems you will endanger the soundness of the breed. In our lifetime we are custodians of the breed for a short time, and we should therefore try to guarantee that future generations have as much pleasure with their dogs as we have.

ENTROPION

This is the in-turning of the margin of one or both eyelids, resulting in the lashes touching the cornea, causing severe irritation. This can be very distressing for your dog, especially in bright sunlight. The rims of the eyes appear to be red and sore and the dog will be in considerable discomfort. An operation is the only way to relieve this problem, but it cannot be regarded as a cure because the condition is hereditary. Leading experts in this field recommend that dogs with this problem should not be used for breeding.

ECTROPION

This is not so common as entropion. It is an outward turning of the margin of the lower lid, on one or both eyes. This leads to inflammation of the eyes, and dogs with this condition may have runny eyes and continuous tear spillage. The treatment and safeguards relating to this condition are the same as for entropion.

DISTICHIASIS

This is a second and abnormal row of lashes, usually incomplete, growing inside the lid margin. This causes irritation of the cornea, which becomes ulcerated. Veterinary treatment is essential. This does not appear to be a problem in Weimaraners at the present time, but a few cases have appeared in recent years. Vigilance is required among all breeders to ensure it does not become a problem in the future.

HIP DYSPLASIA

This hereditary condition can cause a lot of pain to the the animal that is affected. In most cases, the head of the long bone of the leg – the femur – is malformed and does not fit into the pelvic socket properly. This can result in abnormal wear on the sockets. The best safeguard is to have your dogs X-rayed under the Kennel Club B.V.A./H.D. scheme. The hips are checked for wear on the sockets and, and a score is given according to the soundness of the pelvic region – 0 0 being a perfect hip score. Breeders should only use dogs and bitches with low scores. At present, there are insufficient dogs being X-rayed compared to the number of Weimaraners that are being registered, so it is difficult to obtain a true picture of the extent of this problem in the breed.

INTERSEXUALITY

There have been several cases of this condition in the last nine years or so. There is a complete upset in the dog's hormone balance and a bitch may grow dog organs, and vice versa. The Weimaraner Club of Great Britain has been collecting data from some of the litters that have developed this condition, but, to date, there is no concrete evidence to indicate where this problem is coming from.

Appendix

USEFUL ADDRESSES

The Kennel Club
1-5 Clarges Street,
Piccadilly,
London.
WIY 8AB

Tel. 071 493 6651

The Weimaraner Association,
Hon. Sec. Mrs Grace Brown,
Myddlewood Farm,
Myddle,
Nr Shrewsbury,
Shropshire,
SY4 3RY

Tel. 0939 260322

Dog Breeders Associates (puppy lists)
1 Abbey Road,
Bourne End,
Bucks,
SL8 5NZ

Tel. 06285 20943/29000

The Weimaraner Club of Great Britain,
Hon. Sec. Mrs P. LeMon,
6 The Glebe,
Cuxton,
Rochester,
Kent.
ME2 1LW

Tel. 0634 710915

The American Kennel Club,
P51 Madison Avenue,
New York,
N.Y. 10010

Tel. 212 696 8200

The Weimaraner Club of America,
P.O. Box 110708
Nashville,
Tennessee
37222